TREE BARKING

TREE BARKING

A Memoir

NESTA ROVINA

Heyday Books, Berkeley, California
BayTree Books

BAYTREE

This book was made possible in part by a generous grant from the BayTree Fund.

Library of Congress Cataloging-in-Publication Data
Rovina, Nesta.
  Tree barking : a memoir / Nesta Rovina.
    p. ; cm.
  "BayTree books."
  ISBN-13: 978-1-59714-081-2 (pbk. : alk. paper)
  1. Rovina, Nesta. 2. Physical therapists--California--Biography. 3. Occupational therapists--
California--Biography. 4. Home care services--California. I. Title.
  [DNLM: 1. Rovina, Nesta. 2. Home Care Agencies--California. 3. Occupational Therapy-
-California. 4. Community Health Services--California. 5. Personal Narratives--California.
WB 555 R875t 2008]
  RM699.7.R68A3 2008
  615.8'2092--dc22
  [B]
                    2007039604

Cover Photo and Design: Lorraine Rath
Interior Design/Typesetting: Rebecca LeGates
Printing and Binding: Thomson-Shore,
    Dexter, MI

Orders, inquiries, and correspondence should be
addressed to:
  Heyday Books
  P. O. Box 9145, Berkeley, CA 94709
  (510) 549-3564, Fax (510) 549-1889
  www.heydaybooks.com

Printed in the United States of America

10 9 8 7 6 5 4 3 2 1

green press
INITIATIVE

Heyday Books is committed to preserving ancient fores
and natural resources. We elected to print *Tree Barking*
50% post consumer recycled paper, processed chlorine fre
As a result, for this printing, we have saved:

11 Trees (40' tall and 6-8" diameter)
4,450 Gallons of Wastewater
1,790 Kilowatt Hours of Electricity
491 Pounds of Solid Waste
964 Pounds of Greenhouse Gases

Heyday Books made this paper choice because our print
Thomson-Shore, Inc., is a member of Green Press Init
tive, a nonprofit program dedicated to supporting autho
publishers, and suppliers in their efforts to reduce their u
of fiber obtained from endangered forests.

For more information, visit www.greenpressinitiative.or

To my family and friends throughout my personal diaspora

"To be rooted is perhaps the most important and least recognized need of the human soul."—Simone Weil

ACKNOWLEDGMENTS

I would like to thank several people for helping this work come to fruition: William Justice for bringing my work to the attention of Heyday Books; Gayle Wattawa for her invaluable assistance with form and structure; Jeannine Gendar for her patience and scrupulous attention to detail; and all the supportive and competent staff at Heyday. Judy Dodd of Fort Worth, Texas, for putting up with those endless e-mails and for her insightful, not to mention hilarious, comments; Priestess Miriam of New Orleans, who told me I have something to say; the people who shared their stories with me; and my family and friends for your constant support.

CHAPTER 1

I looked at the diagnosis for the fifth time. *Tree barking*. I wondered whether the nurse who had referred me had made a mistake when writing the diagnosis. She had been stressed, but such an error? Surely not. What on earth was "tree barking"? As usual, I had no time to check reference books before leaving the office. I would have to find out later, after work. I find out many things about my patients after work, in medical dictionaries, reference books, obituary columns. I also find out about future patients, usually in a paragraph tucked in somewhere on the back page of a newspaper. For example: "Two people were involved in a drive-by shooting in North Richmond. One was killed and the other, a sixteen-year-old boy, was flown to John Muir Medical Center." I knew that when that boy was released, he would be referred to us.

"Who is it?"

"I'm from the home health agency," I yelled, accustomed to shouting because many of the people I visit are old and hard of hearing.

"I'se comin'."

I waited on the doorstep of the quiet, tree-lined housing complex. I was grateful for the shade; it was a hot, cloudless afternoon. Two young girls about eight and ten years old skipped by, the hem on the younger girl's floral skirt bouncing with each step. They looked at me shyly and smiled.

"You come for Mae?" they asked, bobbing their heads with a click and clack of colorful beads and barrettes.

"Yes," I nodded.

"She be openin' the door soon," they said, waving good-bye.

I heard the door unlatch. The interior of the house was as dark as the face peering at me from that slice of darkness. I pointed to the ID card clipped to my collar.

"I'se sorry I kept you, it's getting harder and harder to walk. Come in, sugar." The woman smiled, her eyes disappearing into the wrinkles lining her forehead and cheeks. Two long, yellow eye teeth framed the space where her front teeth once had been. A red and white bandana was tied around her head. She had a strong voice and sounded as clear as she had on the phone.

She gestured to a well-lived-in armchair upholstered in dark brown corduroy. Using her front-wheeled walker she lumbered slowly and with great difficulty lowered herself onto a chair piled high with cushions. My eyes moved downward over her large, goddess-proportioned body until they remained transfixed on a sight I will never forget. Below her knees her legs ballooned, larger than any swollen legs I'd ever seen. They resembled pictures I had stared at with fascinated horror in medical "freak" books when I was young, only these were far worse. The skin stretched over those calves was gnarled, tough, and furry-looking, full of crevices and nodules, like the bark of an ancient decaying tree. An odor of sweet rotting flesh and decay emanated through the cracks and fissures.

She laced wrinkled fingers together underneath her right upper thigh, just above her right knee. Using her hands as a lever, she heaved, first the right, then the left leg onto a footstool in front of the chair. She shifted her legs until, apparently, she found a position of comfort, turned to me, and displayed a gaptoothed grin.

In her lilting Southern accent, which instantly soothed me, Mae said that recently her legs had become increasingly painful, that she could hardly get in or out of her chair, and as for bathing…

She was not complaining or bemoaning her fate. Mae told me she had good neighbors who, with members of her church, helped her. All she needed was some practical advice in learning how to take care of herself.

While she spoke the odor vanished, replaced by the smell of black-eyed peas and rice simmering on the stove. Her voice dripped like resin from a tree. Lulled by the heat and her voice, I floated to our backyard in South Africa. I leaned against my beloved mulberry tree, reading Enid Blyton's book *The Faraway Tree*, about a wondrous tree growing in an English country garden. The children who lived in the home climbed the tree high, high, high. Once they reached the top they entered the many worlds rotating above the tree and had adventures, exciting, dangerous, and scary. They always managed to escape and descend the tree to the safety of their English country home. I felt the rough bark of the mulberry tree, warmed by the African sun, against my back. A play of dappled light filtered through the leaves and branches. The grass underneath was a lush carpet, warm, green, and soft.

I understood instinctively that despite her pain and discomfort, Mae's legs are a part of her security, her rootedness. They carried her from the South to Richmond during the Second World War. They held her steady as she worked, bore children, and became a part of the community and her church. She has lived in this quiet residential area for many years. She has not disclaimed her legs. Because it is hard for her to leave her home, longtime friends and community members come to help her clean her house and bathe, and to shop for her. Young children drop by to visit, to mow her lawn, and to run errands.

I do not experience this sense of belonging. My own roots remain bleeding and severed in the red South African earth. I have searched for them ever since leaving.

I need to learn to carry mine along with me, as Mae does.

. . .

Just spending an hour with Mae released a flood of memories. With my mind hovering between years and continents, concentrating on traffic, and looking at the signs on the bumpers of passing cars—"Dog Is My Co-Pilot," "My Other Car Is a

Broom"— I drove back to the office. I had to find out what "tree barking" was, as well as finish the evaluation and call her doctor to check whether I could order a tub transfer bench for Mae. This bench has two legs that stand inside the tub, and two outside, so that she could sit on the one end, scoot herself over, and place those enormous and unwieldy legs into water. She would also benefit from a long-handled sponge, in order to easily reach the bottom of her legs and feet to clean them. Later I put samples of these items in my car and took them in for Mae to try. The bench fitted into her bathroom and the tub, and she was delighted by the idea of being able to bathe herself again without needing help from someone else.

Tree barking, I found out, is chronic stasis dermatitis resulting from venous insufficiency. In other words, because of poor circulation, fluids are not pumped back to the heart and lungs, and oxygenated blood does not reach her legs. Edema (swelling) results, causing skin breakdown. It definitely helped to know what her condition was. The next time I saw her, I would show her simple leg exercises to help her circulation.

CHAPTER 2

I would meet a slew of women similar to Mae, strong matri-
archs in a society turned upside down. Although they had
worked their entire lives, many of them were extremely
poor because they mainly worked in the service sectors, as
housecleaners, kitchen workers, maids, and aides. Some had
been abandoned by their men. Others were cared for by their
husbands and families. Some had children who turned to drugs
and crime. No matter their circumstances, they carried on, with
faith, humor, and kindness. So many times, when I meet them,
something about their presence and their acceptance of their lot
in life reminds of my nanny, Betty.

My thoughts float back to South Africa. Tied in a blanket,
snug against Betty's back, I hear the rise and fall of her soothing
voice as she sings softly, and I feel the steady beat of her heart.
Listening to the ancient, life-sustaining rhythm of blood, of
Africa, I am peaceful, warm, and safe.

Betty worked for us from the time I was a toddler. Her
daughter remained in their kraal with her grandparents. Betty
saw her a few times a year, but it felt as if she were showering
the love she had for her daughter upon us. Her husband, Robert,
worked in a factory somewhere in Johannesburg. By law he was
not allowed to live with Betty in the servants' compound, but of
course he visited and most likely stayed overnight. On Saturday nights when my parents went out, they left us with Betty.
Robert and their friends came over and I sat with them in our
kitchen as they played cards and drank endless mugs of sugary,
milky tea. The men nursed bottles of beer between their knees
and rolled dice with a resounding "Hhaa" sound. They spoke
and laughed loudly in their language of rhythms and clicks.

It was Betty who woke us for school, her slippers making a slap-slapping sound as she shuffled into our room, singing softly, "Lazy girl, lazy girl, when the sun was shining, she will lie on the bed like a fool. When they say, 'Let us go to the school,' she say, 'No nana no nana no.'" Still singing, she opened the blinds to let the morning sun stream in. Betty made our breakfast and was in the kitchen when we returned from school. On hot afternoons, when Betty lay resting in her quarters, I sat close to her bed on a wooden chair. I asked her questions about her life before she came to us. What was life like on the kraal? What was her daughter studying? When she came to visit, could Betty's granddaughter also come?

Curiously, one of the things she told me about life on the kraal has always stayed with me. She milked her family's cows and would drink the milk directly from the teat. The way she described the taste of that milk, like creamy warmth, goodness and grass, made an indelible impression on me. When I lived on a kibbutz, the cows were milked by machine, and the milk went into large steel containers before it was pasteurized. On hot summer nights we spooned off the creamy top, unconcerned about bovine TB, and took it back to our room to blend with instant coffee and ice.

Betty taught me the African national anthem, "Nkosi Sikelel' iAfrika." Betty never kicked me out or complained about me being a nuisance. I don't recall Betty complaining about anything; quietly and comfortingly, she was present in our lives. Betty taught me to pay attention to my dreams. She was a runner for "fah-fee," the local gambling game run by a Chinese man. From my dreams Betty discerned symbols, which she translated into numbers, and she placed her money on numbers from one through thirty-six. Sometimes, when I had a dream that inspired her to guess the right number, she shared her winnings with me. My brother, sister, and I felt unconditional love from Betty's constant, warm, loving presence. We were devastated when she became ill with cancer and returned to her kraal. Betty died at the age of thirty-nine.

. . .

I remember one night at the Berkeley Repertory Theater. A South African friend and I went to see Athol Fugard's play *"Master Harold"...and the Boys*. Afterward there was a dialogue between him and members of the audience.

"What is it like growing up as a white South African?" someone asked him.

What would he respond, my friend and I wondered, as we looked at each other with pleasure at the sound of his familiar accent.

"That is different for everyone," he replied, "but there is something universal to almost every white South African. We are all raised by a loving black presence. One day we become aware that we are the masters of that presence, and that is a traumatic event for us."

My entire life was dominated by the brutal system of apartheid. Apartheid is an Afrikaans word meaning "separateness," which formed the basis of the policies of the Nationalist government. All the inhabitants of South Africa were separated according to racial classification. We took many things for granted: having servants, separate buses and transport, separate entries into homes, buildings, and offices, separate beaches, separate amenities (lesser or none for the blacks, or coloreds). But I remember being horrified by the ways in which people were segregated, brutalized, and mistreated, simply because of the color of their skin.

All of these things were apartheid, separateness, and it had always been like that, ever since I could remember. What made things horrible for me was, for instance, the time when Stanley, our male servant, went to fetch the morning paper from the gate at the bottom of our garden. He did this every morning, but one morning he didn't come back. No one knew where he was. Later that day my father received a call from the police asking if a certain Stanley Mafekeng worked for us. "Yes," said my father. "Then come and get him," said the policeman. My father went to the Old Fort in Johannesburg and found Stanley, bleeding and badly bruised. When my father, a lawyer, asked what crime he had committed, the policeman on duty replied that he did not have his passbook on him when he was at the bottom of the driveway.

That morning, apparently, when confronted by the police, Stanley told them his passbook was in his room in the servants' quarters in the backyard of our house, but they would not allow him to get it. Instead they treated quiet and shy Stanley like a criminal. They beat him up and took him away, only bothering to call my father much later, after the fact.

I felt guilty and ashamed of what white people did, yet I was one of them.

How sad, to grow up a stranger in my own country, but what I did not realize was just how firmly my heart was anchored to this land, like an umbilical cord that can never be severed. I did not know that growing up in those circumstances would establish a pattern that would accompany me always, that of feeling both a participant and a stranger. I have experienced this duality everywhere I have lived—South Africa, Israel, America—no matter for how long, or what events have happened: I always feel somewhat apart, my own internal apartheid. Certainly it has made me acutely aware of the subtle and not so subtle ways in which discrimination is played out, both externally and internally, and how all of us are participants.

CHAPTER 3

"Pásale" (come in), said a young woman with a shy smile and masses of shiny, thick, brown hair that hung down her back in a ropey braid. She opened her door to let me into a home smelling strongly of Pine-Sol.

Rosa was all of seventeen. She and her husband, whom I never met because he was always out working, lived together in one room of a home in Richmond. Extended family members shared this home, but the lives of this couple and their nine-month-old son were confined to their room and the kitchen. Their first child had been referred to us because he was born with not one, but several debilitating syndromes that affected the bones of his head as well as his heart and skeletal system. Their small room consisted of a large chest of drawers purchased from a nearby flea market, where they also bought a twin-size bed, the obligatory TV, and a stroller for the infant. Over the bed was a large wooden cross, and next to it a calendar with an image of Jesus. Small suitcases and packets of diapers were neatly placed underneath their rack of clothing in the closet. The little boy lay in their bed. Next to it was a car seat for those times he spent out of bed.

I really understood this young woman, all alone in a country to which she had come because of her husband. Now they had a son with multiple handicaps and her husband worked all day, came back for dinner in the evenings, then went to the local gym to work out. She did not know English, and their young boy was not okay. How did she cope, all alone, without any resources?

At the age of twenty, I left South Africa for Israel. In retrospect this seems so very young, but at the time I felt I was a mature woman. For a couple of years I learned Hebrew and worked in Tel Aviv, but my ever present desire to travel pushed me onward to Europe, then back to Israel. Upon my return I fell in love with a South African man. Raymond, like me, had left South Africa to make a home in Israel.

Together we moved to a kibbutz in the beautiful Jezreel Valley, in the lower Galilee, where we married one crystal-clear spring night. The sounds of laughter, music, and the clinking of wine glasses, and the intoxicating perfume of night-blooming jasmine, filled the fresh night air. How happy we were underneath the canopy of the star-laden sky, how full of promises—our future unfurled, like an undulating veil, before us. We would travel, have children. I would study. I had not yet decided what, but time was on our side. We would grow old together.

Thank goodness our futures are mercifully obscured; otherwise, would any of us embark on anything? A few months after we were married, I became happily pregnant. However, almost immediately after discovering this I began spotting, pinprick red dots, and I was placed on bed rest, permitted only to shower and use the toilet. All seemed fine until one Saturday evening, a few weeks later, when the tiny red spots reappeared, increasing in size and intensity until the pregnancy had to be terminated.

We did not know that this was just a foreshadowing of far worse events. Pregnant again in July, I started bleeding again. This time Ray was in the army, somewhere down in the Sinai Peninsula. Once more, I was placed on bed rest. I was scared to move, petrified that maybe my getting up to bathe and use the toilet had caused my first miscarriage. I felt helpless. Although I was young and healthy, I was unable to move about our tiny room, and I was totally dependent on others. A woman whose duty it was to look after the sick and bedridden came by every day, brought me food, tidied our room, and helped me sponge bathe. Friends flitted through, making tea, bringing flowers and the latest gossip. I was bedridden for three months. I watched the shadows as the sun moved from east to west and learned to tell the time without looking at my watch. This did not make

me feel closer to nature, it was an act of desperation. Sometimes I noticed a spot on the wall that I could have wiped off,
had I been able to get up, and helplessly I watched as the spot
grew into an unsightly blotch, spilling over into my room and
my surroundings. Because of the unrelenting heat I was always
thirsty, and the fact that I could not even get up to pour myself a
glass of water reduced me to bouts of crying. I had endless time
to feel sorry for myself, so I requested work. The lady brought
clothing from the communal laundry that needed mending
and folding. Doing something useful helped me tremendously,
somehow even diminishing the size of the blotch on the wall.

I miscarried anyway, but as sad and empty as I felt, I had
learned the value of making a contribution to the community,
no matter how small—and also, the importance of allowing
people to help me.

CHAPTER 4

On the 6th of October, 1973, not long after my second miscarriage, I awoke to the pounding of hammers. I was excited because I knew Ray would be back for good the next weekend; his six months of service were over. Turning over in bed, I remembered today was Yom Kippur, the Day of Atonement. I joined the young people who were building a *succa,* a temporary shelter in which we would eat for a week to remind ourselves of the impermanence of our time on earth. We planned a large welcome-home party for Ray on the following Friday evening. It would be held at the pool, complete with music, drink, food, and dancing.

On the secular kibbutz in which we lived, Yom Kippur was not observed. Certainly no one fasted. After an early lunch, a group of us went to the pool. It was a lazy day, a day to do nothing but lie together in a heap on the cropped grass, arms on legs, heads on soft stomachs, legs on legs, smoking, touching, laughing. There was nothing to listen to except the sensual strains of Arabic songs on the Arabic radio stations. Hebrew radio stations were closed because of Yom Kippur.

At precisely two o' clock, two Mirage planes screeched upward, ripping the silence apart. They vanished, leaving trails of white vapor in their wake.

"How strange," I said to a friend. "Planes on Yom Kippur."

An older man rode by on his bicycle, holding a radio to his ear. He skidded to a halt in front of us, using his feet as brakes. Holding the bike steady with one hand, the radio in the other, he said, "Go to your rooms, turn on your radios. There is a war."

In unison we stood up and silently walked to our bedrooms. Everyone knew Ray was in the Sinai, and they gravitated to our

room. We turned on the radio: "Israel has been attacked on
all fronts. There is to be a total blackout: tape your windows,
keep buckets of water in your rooms. Black out the headlights
on your cars." Men in khaki uniforms arrived at the kibbutz in
jeeps, in buses, in cars, to fetch the men in their units. How do
you say good-bye to a man going to war?

Raymond was killed that day, at four o'clock in the afternoon.
The Egyptians fired missiles into their bunker, Budapest, the
northernmost outpost along the supposedly impregnable Bar
Lev line. Six soldiers were killed there on the first day, Raymond
one of them. I did not learn of his death until ten days later.

And so, like the appearance of the Mirages in the sky at two
o'clock on the Day of Atonement, like a bolt of lightning, our
lives changed forever. My new life began that day, with new
memories, alone, nothing shared. The dead must be buried. Life
must go on. In accordance with Jewish custom, those soldiers
killed in the Sinai would be buried in a "grave of brothers" at
Kibbutz Beeri, in the Negev. On the day of the funeral, in late
October, I went to Kibbutz Beeri with my family and some
members of the kibbutz. Five hundred soldiers were buried that
day. The cease-fire had been broken, the fighting had resumed.

As we approached Kibbutz Beeri, hollow sounds, like the
beating of drums, grew louder. We parked in the dusty parking grounds, alongside hundreds of other cars. The air was rent
with unearthly wails and shrieks. Weakly, I looked around and
saw masses of people, old and young, black and white, poor and
rich, men, women, and children. Some stumbled in the dust,
beating on their breasts, screaming to a God who did not hear.
Some staggered, clinging to each other. Others walked upright,
alone, mouths tightly clenched. Inside the cemetery were row
upon row of simple graves. Oblongs of gravel, each with a
simple stick, painted white, placed in the middle. On each stick
the name of the soldier and his military number were neatly
printed in black lettering. I stared at Ray's number. I stared at
the gravel. Was he underneath? This white stick, these stones,
they had nothing to do with the man I loved—the man with

whom I had laughed, cried, and fought, with whom I had made love. The young man with the firm, slim, warm body, the thick, curly, dark brown hair, the deep, wise, velvet eyes.

I spent that night with my parents, who had immigrated to Israel three years before. I pulled a pillow over my head in a feeble attempt to dull the sounds of the screaming. Sometime during that dreadful night, along with the noise of my thoughts and images of graves and white sticks, I remembered the feelings of fulfillment I had experienced working during the months of bed rest. The next morning I stumbled into the kitchen to find my mother standing next to the sink, washing dishes. An apron decorated with South African flowers was tied around her waist. Steam rose from the kettle. She turned to greet me.

"I'm going to study occupational therapy," I said, surprising both her and myself.

I realized then, at the tender age of twenty-six, that life is random and unfair, no one is immune from suffering. I thought that the least I could do was assist my fellow travelers, be of service, and alleviate suffering, even if only for a brief while.

CHAPTER 5

And now, many years and journeys later, here I stand in Richmond, California, in front of Rosa, a devastated young girl whose life had also been full of promises. Besides gaining her confidence and trust, and showing her how to help her child in his development, I listen to her, allow her to laugh and cry, help decipher medical notices, and explain the intricacies of BART, the San Francisco Bay Area's transit system. I find a free support group for young immigrant women exactly in her position: alone, frightened, isolated. I encourage her to go to English as Second Language classes so she can find work and maybe get an education. Years later I saw Rosa working as a cashier in a deli. She had learned English and, most importantly, her son was doing well.

. . .

Although I remained a member of the kibbutz, I lived in Jerusalem, where I studied occupational therapy for three years. OTs (the acronym for occupational therapists) assist people who have been ill or are disabled, physically or mentally, to return to their former level of function, and to be as independent as possible in their activities of daily living—for example, to get out of bed, go to the toilet, bathe, and brush one's teeth. These are the basics we all take for granted until for some reason, be it of disease or trauma, we can no longer do them.

I attended classes in Hadassah Hospital, on Mt. Scopus in Jerusalem. These were intense, six days a week from early morning to late in the evening. Anatomy, physiology, psychology, sociology, kinesiology, pathology, neurology, as well as crafts such as carpentry, weaving, and ceramics: not only were these subjects new to me, but everything was in Hebrew, so it was doubly difficult. However, to my pleasant surprise, I received my degree and learned Hebrew really well.

I worked as an occupational therapist in a large hospital near the kibbutz, and in a senior citizens' home. In fact, I was doing what I had always dreamed of since moving with Ray to the kibbutz—living on it but doing what I wanted to do elsewhere, so that I did not feel stifled. It was then that I realized I had another pattern, besides one of feeling apart. Once I achieved my dreams, new ones began to foment. My dormant desire for travel, as well as the need for change, began to well up inside. I knew that the time had come to leave the kibbutz and begin something new. It was at this juncture that my brother came to Israel for a visit. He opened a door for me by inviting me to study yoga in the Bahamas, where he was living. And so I embarked on a journey that took me from Israel to the Bahamas, and eventually to California.

Thirteen years later, I found myself living in Oakland, California. I had completed a master's degree but worked in various meaningless positions because I was too scared to commit to anything, always living with the underlying thought that I would be on the move again—and if I ever did commit to anything, or anyone, it would all be taken away again. Besides, I wanted the time and the freedom to be creative. However, when I had time and freedom I did not have money, and my creative juices froze from the constant dread of not being able to pay rent. It took the combination of living hand to mouth and the powers of persuasion of an occupational therapist I knew to get me to return to the profession.

CHAPTER 6

I began working for Contra Costa County's home health agency in 1992. As a home health therapist I work with patients who are deemed homebound, either by virtue of their illness or because it would be too taxing for them to leave their homes for medical treatment, such as occupational or physical therapy.

I remember an ad I saw for home health workers, in which a spanking clean car was parked under the shade of a gracious elm tree outside a tastefully painted home. A smiling therapist, wearing a starched white jacket over neatly pressed pants, stepped out of her clean, late-model car. Waiting for her on the porch stood an attractive, well-dressed couple. The woman held a poodle close to her chest. After my first day on the job I had an inkling that this may have been a misrepresentation, and I hoped I would be strong enough for the challenges ahead.

How clearly I remember that first day, commuting from Oakland to the county health clinic in Concord. At the time I began this job, I lived in North Oakland. I left for work in the early morning. In the summertime Oakland is often shrouded in a cool layer of fog. Outside was downright cold, and I wore a warm jacket over my T-shirt. I drove a Toyota Corolla that did not have air conditioning. I hadn't needed it when I bought the car, because on the two or so hot days a year, I simply opened the windows; on cool and misty mornings I turned up the heat and set off for work.

Highway 24's Caldecott Tunnel bores through the East Bay hills to Contra Costa County. I joined the herd of cars shuffling along, bumper to bumper, through the tunnel in a kind of ritualistic birth passage. An unrelentingly blue, cloudless sky and a mercilessly hot sun beat down as I emerged on the other side of the tunnel. The climate was apparently frying brains, causing the population to behave differently from people on the cooler side of the hills. Cars transformed into fast-flying pickup trucks driven by young, fair-haired boys wearing baseball caps with the visors turned down the backs of their heads. They drove swiftly, weaving between lanes. Sleek, tanned, perky young women with straight blonde hair drove without apparent regard for anyone else on the crowded freeways. No one seemed to know, or care, that the right-hand lane is for slower-moving traffic.

I stepped into a room crowded with women, only women it seemed, although later I did notice at least two men. They all sat at desks crammed tightly against each other. I learned they were nurses, interpreters, social workers, home health aides, a physical therapist, and an occupational therapist. Some worked full-time, some part-time, and some per diem. The one trait they shared was that they appeared harried, riffling through piles of paperwork on their desks with one hand, holding phones to their ears in the other, and shouting into earpieces held in place by a raised shoulder and a neck cocked to the side, a precursor of future problems. They made notes in appointment books, or on the many sheets of paper strewn all over the desks and piled high onto shelves above them. Pictures of spouses and children were displayed on surfaces not covered with paper. Whose picture would I put up, I wondered. Maybe postcards from South Africa and Israel?

I spent a week learning the most important aspect of home health in America, paperwork: how to fill in endless amounts of paperwork, including time sheets, daily mileage, evaluations of patients, progress notes, requests to doctors and medical supply companies, and so on, ad nauseum. Completing paperwork, it seemed, was far more important than time spent with patients. All of this was to satisfy the insurance companies whom we billed for our services. At first I thought I would never manage, but I reminded myself that if I had studied in Hebrew, I could learn to do paperwork here in America.

During the first week I also accompanied my supervisor on visits. We drove out to see a man who lived with his wife way out on the 680 freeway. He was recovering from a stroke. Seeing them in their surroundings reminded me of how, when I first came to America, it seemed that everything was just like in the movies. This couple lived in an unnecessarily large suburban home. They were getting ready to barbecue unnecessarily large steaks which sat, raw and bloody, on a chopping board on the counter. Their entire home, or the areas I saw—the living room, kitchen, and bathroom—were all decorated in Elvis memorabilia. Elvis was even straddling the light switches. This was neither the layout nor the decor I had known in homes in South Africa and Israel.

Working in home health, I soon realized, is somewhat like looking at snapshots of a person's life. I get to see people at a certain juncture and spend a short time with them, then my work is finished. Often I will never know the end results, unless, as sometimes happens, I bump into them or a member of their family, or the patient is referred again at a later date. By then they are usually worse off than they were the first time I saw them.

The agency receives referrals from doctors, public health nurses, physical therapists, and discharge planners in hospitals. We, the rehabilitation workers, are sent to homes to assess the condition of our patients and develop treatment plans. These plans usually entail exercises to strengthen weakened limbs and other measures to ensure that patients are safe and independent in their home settings. I instruct patients, or their families and caregivers, or both. Sometimes their safety requires the use of special equipment, a bedside commode or a tub transfer bench, for example, so I carry samples of different items in my car.

This work requires many skills, not the least of which is the ability to read a map, a skill I have never acquired. In Israel, a person who is a little "different" is said to have lost his or her north. Indeed, ever since leaving South Africa, my internal world, like my outer physical world, is jumbled. I cannot distinguish between north, south, east, and west, but somehow, by sheer instinct and luck, I usually arrive at the correct address. This is fortunate, as in most places where I work it is not advisable to either look lost or to ask for directions. This is what the other workers told me, and I soon found out why.

CHAPTER 7

Prior to beginning my work in Contra Costa County, my knowledge of the Bay Area was confined to Alameda County, in which I lived and worked, and San Francisco and Marin County. I visited friends in Mendocino and went down south to Big Sur and the Zen Buddhist Retreat Center, Tassajara, but other than forays to Orinda, where I studied, and to Walnut Creek to visit family, I was quite unaware of Contra Costa County. It is a large county of sharp contrasts: extreme wealth and extreme poverty, urban sprawl, farmlands, suburbs, inner cities, beautiful regional parks, golf courses, country clubs, and oil refineries.

Just east of the Caldecott Tunnel lie the towns of Orinda, Moraga, Lafayette, Walnut Creek, and Pleasant Hill. Concord, too, is situated in this region known as "Central County." Further south are Danville, Blackhawk, San Ramon, and other rapidly growing areas. For the most part, the population in these areas appears affluent. Lovely homes, sometimes built from indigenous redwood, nestle among the tawny, rolling hills of central and eastern Contra Costa County. The nonstop California sunshine streams through large glass windows that afford expansive vistas of hills and open space, shaded by groves of sycamore, oak, and walnut trees.

Blackhawk is a gated community set in the middle of nowhere, along the 680 freeway. My fellow workers told me about its beautiful mansions, and I looked forward to seeing them. I tootled along the freeway in my old, gray, dented Corolla with the windows rolled down, allowing the hot, dry air to blow through. The first time I went there was toward the end of August, and the grassy verges were brittle and straw-colored, burned dry after the long hot summer.

As I neared Blackhawk, off to my right was a lake surrounded by well-manicured green grass. Ducks paddled idly around. I realized the lake and grass were artificial and wondered vaguely about the ducks. Following the directions on my referral, I turned right and drove down the wide avenue that led to the gate. The security guard eyed my car, his face registering disdain. I told him whom I had come to see. He checked my ID and called the family, then waved me through. No cars were parked on the streets, but BMW's, Mercedes Benzes, Jeeps, and the ubiquitous four-wheel-drive pickups whizzed silently by. Visors protected the drivers' perfectly tanned faces from the sun. If urban necessities such as laundromats, corner coffeehouses, bookstores, or curbside recycling existed, they were cunningly disguised. Mansions built in pseudo-Tudor, pseudo-Mediterranean, and other pseudo styles, surrounded by large expanses of lush green lawns, looked incongruous in the surrounding arid land.

These areas, in their surface blandness, reminded me of the South African suburbs in which I grew up. The occupants also appeared bland, boring and smug in their spacious cocoons of security and prosperity.

Western Contra Costa County consists of El Cerrito, Richmond, San Pablo, El Sobrante, Pinole, Rodeo, Crockett, Hercules, and Martinez. Kensington also constitutes a part of western Contra Costa County. It is its own enclave, a sort of bubble which appears as an English idyll of large homes surrounded by colorful gardens with a staid "downtown" of pubs, butchers, and curiosity shoppes, and a golf course. Some of the other places, with their extremely low incomes, high rates of unemployment, and attendant crime, offer a direct contrast to Central County. Many communities lie in the shadow of the large refineries, and it is probably not coincidental that there is a disproportionately high rate of cancer, asthma, and pulmonary disease in these areas.

CHAPTER 8

Concord consists of shopping malls, modern office buildings of glass, artificial fountains, wide avenues lined with car dealerships, identical townhouses, apartment buildings, and ranch-style housing developments. On the surface, the impression is that of a predominantly white, conservative population. In reality the population is mixed and includes Blacks, Russians, Afghanis, East Indians, Latinos, and Asians.

One of my first visits to Concord was to a young woman who suffered from seizures and a rare bone disease that caused her bones to break easily. Together these are a lethal combination. The people who suffer from this rare genetic disease are not the kind of people one can hug heartily, or slap on the back in a hail-fellow-well-met kind of way: such a gesture may crack the bones in their fragile skeletal systems.

I planned to instruct her in home safety to prevent further broken bones, especially in the shower. When I arrived she told me her roommate was using the shower. In the meantime I examined the two-bedroom apartment for safety hazards. I suggested she remove her throw rugs because, pretty as they were, none of them had any backing, and to trip on one could be fatal. I recommended fastening down the many computer and phone cords which slunk in snakelike patterns over the living room carpets into the bedroom and down the hallway, disappearing under her roommate's door.

Her artwork covered the walls of the living room: intricate, mandala-like paintings of people who resembled fantastic-looking animals, drawn with felt-tip pens in vivid greens, oranges, yellows, and reds. The total effect was somewhat disturbing. It seemed the electrical currents which fired at inappropriate intervals in her brain caused her to see the world rather like Van Gogh on a mixture of absinthe and acid.

I asked her how it felt spending one's life inside an eggshell. She told me she had suffered deep depressions, and despair, but new medications seemed to be helping. Her seizures had abated, and she no longer felt so exhausted and anxious. She planned to make postcards of her artwork. In fact, she hoped to set up a small stationery business in her home.

At least half an hour had passed. I glanced in the direction of the shower. I did not hear any water running.

"She takes forever," the woman said. "You can ask her to hurry."

I knocked on the bathroom door and asked whether I could use the bathroom for just a few minutes.

"No problem," answered a man's voice.

I thought I'd heard the patient saying, "She takes a long time to get ready."

The bathroom door opened and a waft of heady perfume emanated from inside. I tried to act as if nothing was out of the ordinary when a purple creature floated out. It was a he in the throes of transforming into a she. Purple was his color of choice: purple shoes, purple lingerie, purple eye shadow, purple earrings. He held a blonde wig in his hand. His own hair, or rather, the stray wisps that remained visible, was dark brown.

"Sorry," I said, hoping I didn't look as shocked as I felt. "I just need the bathroom for a few minutes."

"No problem," he said in a deep voice that then changed into a falsetto. "I can finish in my bedroom." He smiled and winked as he sashayed past.

My goodness, I thought, where can things go from here?

CHAPTER 9

At the time I was hired, in 1992, my supervisor told me that working for the county was really secure. Most of the workers, she said, had been with the county for years, decades even. In fact, many couples worked in the different sectors of the county government, enjoying their combined benefits and future retirement plans. A severe recession had just begun, however, and soon we would all feel the effects.

Because Contra Costa County is widespread, the homes are often long distances from one another, so I tried to plan my day around patients who lived fairly close to each other. For example, when I worked out of the Concord office, I would begin by visiting people as close to Concord as possible, then drive westward, on to Martinez, San Pablo, and Richmond. This route brought me closer to Alameda County, where I lived, thus preventing an arduous commute back from Concord.

The county had offices and clinics in Concord, Martinez, Richmond, and Pittsburg. I mostly worked in the central and western areas of the county, but I would also go further east, to Pittsburg, Antioch, Oakley, Brentwood, and neighboring communities. Sometimes I worked out of the Richmond office, beginning my day in North Richmond, an unincorporated area. Not only is it a high crime area, but the residents are also plagued by cancer and respiratory problems, especially asthma, because of diesel exhaust from freight trains, industry, and the monster trucks that rumble along Interstate 80 to Interstate 580, spewing poisons onto the residents. The old homes have lead in the paint and in the soil. The babies eat it and suffer from high levels of lead in their blood, which causes neurological illnesses, retardation, and even delinquency. Because of the drug dealing and attendant crime, it is advisable to begin work early, before the dealers and users begin their daily hustle of selling, buying, and using.

. . .

One of my first visits to North Richmond was to an old woman who had suffered a stroke. Because of the dire warnings from everyone in the Concord office, I felt apprehensive following the referring nurse's directions down a potholed street. And just before I had left the office, a home health aide who lived in North Richmond had asked me where I was going. After she heard the address, she told me to keep my doors locked and my windows shut, and to drive away if anyone came close to my car.

I passed a mom-and-pop store, but mom and pop must have left years before. The walls were covered in graffiti—red, blue, and black slashes that appeared angry and random. It was only years later that I started being able to discern gang tags in the seeming chaos. A pay phone had been ripped from the outside wall. The wire hung down, like a headless snake. Despite the heat, a large number of youths, wearing oversize black jackets and black knitted caps with the white initials of the New York Yankees emblazoned in front, milled about the outside of the store and spilled onto the street, which was littered with broken bottles, cigarette butts, wrappers, discarded clothing, plastic bags, and other debris. They didn't seem to look at my car or me. I came to a street near the store where I thought I should turn left, but there was no street name. I turned left anyway and drove to the end of the block, on which stood nothing but a few boarded-up houses. I turned left, left again, and found myself passing the store again. This time I thought I saw a couple of the young men look at my car, but I wasn't sure—anyway, what difference did it make? Two more rutted streets, still no names. I drove around a couple more unnamed streets, until I realized I was lost. My map was of no help (even though I can't read maps, I can locate street names on them). Only afterward I learned that it was because I had looked up streets in Richmond, not North Richmond. The only people I had seen on the streets were in the vicinity of the mom-and-pop store. I wondered whether there was a working phone inside. I could go in, but that would mean parking and walking through the young men milling outside. Maybe I should ask them for the street?

An incident that had occurred many years before surprised me by pushing its unwelcome way upward from the depths of my being. It had happened in Johannesburg one hot December evening. It was on that evening that my liberal sentiments were severely challenged.

As whites in South Africa, we were raised with a dread of *"die swart gevaar"* (the black peril). We were made to understand that unless the policies of apartheid were strictly enforced, we, the beleaguered whites, would eventually be slaughtered by hordes of wild blacks. My parents belonged to the Liberal Party, and every night over dinner they told us to ignore that frightening image, because it was nothing but a scare tactic. Instead, my father said, the ever stricter and unjust rules of apartheid may eventually cause a revolution. Hopefully, the situation would change before judgment day.

On the day of the incident, it is very hot; the fiery orange ball that is the sun is on its way down, dark comes swiftly. I am nineteen years old and am a fairly new driver. I am alone in the car with all the windows rolled down so that something resembling a breeze can flow over me. Because of the "so hot you can fry an egg on the pavement" heat, and because it is almost Christmas and the black servants have nowhere else to go, they congregate on the pavements and street corners, drinking and playing music on pennywhistles and guitars fashioned out of empty petrol cans and string. I see a crowd of them, "die swart gevaar," as I approach a traffic light. I pray the light will change to green and I won't have to stop, and, because my heart has begun beating faster I realize I am scared. The men hold knobkerries in their hands (wooden sticks with a round knob carved on top). They pass bottles between them, some staggering, some dancing, shouting "happy, happy" as they swig from the bottle. The light is still red. The men surround my car, hitting it with their knobkerries and laughing. In reality they tap the car lightly, but in my mind I hear earsplitting blows, glass shattering and metal breaking. They chant and sing in Zulu. I cannot understand a word of what are probably the latest popular songs, but I am sure these are war cries. In those seconds, as my heart jumps into my mouth and, despite the heat, my flesh grows clammy and cold, I understand the government. They are scared, and their policies reflect this terror. In my own fear and panic I feel a hot bubble of anger exploding inside of me and shove the car into first gear, step hard on the accelerator, release the clutch, and drive off, not caring about the red light or whether I hit someone. "The government is right, we should kill them all," I think blindly, angrily, as I drive away, gripping the steering wheel tightly.

In bed that night I thought of my reaction and was deeply ashamed. I realized how eroding it is to grow up under oppression and fear. Everyone becomes a victim. That incident was yet another notch I mentally carved as a reason to leave the country.

Remembering this, I again drew close to the store and the young men. This time I was relieved to see a sheriff's car. I stuck my hand through the window and flagged him down. He stopped alongside of me. His window shooshed down electronically.

"What the hell are you doing here?" were his first polite and calming words.

I smiled, showed him my county ID, and gave him the name of the street I was looking for. Instead of giving me directions, he barked, "They send you out here? What the hell? Do you know there are no police around here? If you get into trouble, you are on your own. No law enforcement people are gonna come down here. No ma'am, you're on your own."

He closed his window more than halfway and put his hands on the wheel. An interested crowd gathered a few feet further down the road. He was so nice to me, this sheriff, that I shuddered at the thought of how he must have addressed the young men when he had occasion to.

I swallowed hard and repeated my request for the directions.

Grudgingly, he told me where to go, shot me a withering look, and drove away.

The street was, in fact, right where I had been, but the sign had been ripped off. The old woman I came to see sat on the porch in an armchair, smiling and nodding at her husband and grandson sitting on a bench opposite her. They held her hand and patted her affectionately while I sat with them, asking questions. She had suffered a stroke, which left her with a weak right arm and leg and unable to speak. I showed them how to help her out of the chair by stabilizing their knees against hers, so they could help her to stand without having to lean forward and hurt their backs. Using cans of food I found in the kitchen, I demonstrated arm exercises. Then together, with her using her walker, we went to the toilet and I showed her how to sit without fear of falling. I brought my bath bench into their home, set it over the bath, and showed her how to transfer to the bench from the walker. When she tried the same transfer alone and discovered she could slide in and out of the bath herself, she was delighted. A smile spread over the left side of her face and she beamed in the direction of her husband and grandson.

CHAPTER 10

"Bleak" was the first word that came into my mind when I entered some of the areas where I worked. It repeated itself, mantra-like, bleak, bleak, bleak. In fact, sometimes the homes and the surroundings are downright depressing. The first time I went to South Richmond, to the home of a woman who'd had a hip replacement, the rain had been coming down in torrents for days. Street drainage was clogged with leaves, candy wrappers, crumpled paper bags, plastic bags, chicken bones, half eaten slices of bread, used condoms, and water collected in deep, dirty puddles. Yellow street signs were barely discernible through the rain, and also because of the graffiti slashed on them. But I deciphered DIP in large black letters. Indeed, my car dipped through about two feet of water each time I came to a crossing. To my infinite relief, it never stalled or stopped. Because of the inclement weather, no one was outside.

When I opened my car door I heard loud voices. They came from the parking lot of an apartment a couple of houses away. A group of young black guys, all wearing baggy hooded sweatshirts, were conversing. Curse words punctuated each word. The house I had to go to stood back from the street in a tiny yard. As I walked to the door, on my right-hand side stood two overflowing garbage cans. Scraps of iron and steel were strewn on the ground nearby. Iron bars covered the door and windows. I rattled the bars and banged, calling the patient's name. Two Dobermans jumped from behind the neighbor's fence, baring their teeth and barking. Thank goodness they were on leashes. So much for the photo of the friendly little dog in the nice couple's arms in the ad for a home health occupational therapist. No one replied, even though I knocked several times. I returned to my car. The young guys were still conversing loudly. I called the patient from my car phone. She answered and said that no one had heard any knocking, but someone would open the door.

An extremely tall, stooped, emaciated man with gray hair, dark sallow skin, and watery blue eyes opened the door and ushered me in. The place was dark. I stumbled over empty soda cans, newspapers strewn all over, ashtrays overflowing with cigarette stubs, phone cords, plates of dog food, and the inner cardboard tubes of toilet paper until I reached a room where a cheery-looking lady in her forties sat on the edge of a bed. The sheets were stained and bore scorch marks of cigarettes, and what surely were bits of dried feces. Her chirpy demeanor was in total contrast to the squalid conditions.

She was an attractive woman, possibly of Pacific Island descent. Her skin was a beautiful coppery bronze and she had a thick head of wavy, dark brown hair. She suffered some type of weak bone condition and apparently had just undergone a second hip replacement surgery. Because this was her second surgery, I knew she would know how to use a bath bench. She must have received a bench or stool after her first operation. "Yes," she said, she knew how to use it and would like one. It was too much to hope that she might have kept hers—I wouldn't have either, I don't like reminders of illnesses or surgeries. She pointed in the direction of the bathroom so I could check whether a bench would fit. The stench emanating from the room was overwhelming, and I dry-heaved. Someone's or some animal's feces were smeared on the floor of the room and the tub. When I returned to the bedroom, she cheerily pushed aside the gray, filthy sheets to make a place for me to sit, but I told her I preferred to stand, as I sat in my car so much. What could I really say? "There is no way I would sit on that bed of yours without being able to bathe immediately afterward, preferably in disinfectant"?

I had no idea of the role the man played—father, lover, landlord? He remained standing in the room, peering at us through rheumy eyes, occasionally grunting his assent about something. They both chain-smoked. He ground his butts out on the carpet, and she stubbed hers into an ashtray, the contents of which overflowed onto the bed and carpet.

In South Africa our homes were clean. Granted, we had armies of servants to keep them in such spanking condition, but the servants' tiny rooms were spotless too. We visited a kraal not far from Johannesburg on a school outing, and the inside of the small, round huts was spic-and-span. The sweet-smelling floors were smeared with cow dung daily to keep away insects, then swept out. Straw mats were rolled up neatly in the hut. Betty's tiny room was never dirty or in disarray. How could people live in such filth? I pondered how environment affects state of mind, or vice versa.

I completed my evaluation, knowing I would have to return to this place after I ordered the bath bench.

The next and last time I went was on a clear, sunny day. As I neared the home, I felt I had entered what Tibetan Buddhists would call a bardo, a transitional place between lives, in this case a gateway to hell. Potholes, like pockmarks, dotted the road. Men, women, and children crowded around street corners. Some were scrawny and staggered around aimlessly. Cars burned rubber, and the steamy air vibrated with insistent, heavy bass beats. A young boy lay on the steps of a building, holding his head. The two Dobermans, like the gatekeepers of Hades, were there to greet me.

CHAPTER 11

This work would have been far more stressful, difficult, depressing, and alienating if it were not for the fact that I met my coworkers in the office, usually at the beginning and end of each day. My fellow workers were as varied as the patients, and for me, telling stories and listening to their jokes or advice was a way of letting off steam, or venting frustration.

The rehabilitation supervisor for the occupational therapists and physical therapists worked mostly out of the Concord office, so many of our interactions were over the phone. This was just as well, because she constantly clicked her pen and jiggled her ankle, two habits that drove me crazy. As she was the supervisor, she only made a few home visits. She was an OT by training, and she went on visits when the other OT and I had too many patients to manage or were not working. On those occasions, we noticed that she included what seemed to be an unnecessarily large number of visits in her treatment plans. None of us had time to go out and see anyone two or three times a week, especially as we only worked twenty hours, officially. But, of course, insurance companies were billed for these visits, and the home health agency would show a profit.

The clicking of her pen and jiggling of her ankle notwithstanding, she was blessed with a wonderful sense of humor, and we spent many pleasant times together laughing over "battle stories."

In the office were nurses, the nursing supervisor, and the home health aides, who went to patients' homes to bathe them, assist with meal setup, and help with exercise programs. One of the nurses was a large, burly looking man of Irish heritage. He sported a snake earring in one ear and always wore alligator boots. At first he looked intimidating, but in fact he was one the gentlest, kindest, and funniest men I've known. He was not at all reticent about his past, which included service in Vietnam, alcoholism and heroin addiction, overdoses, and work in many different settings, including orthopedic wards, psychiatric wards, and drug rehabilitation centers. He was not healthy, suffering from high blood pressure and diabetes. Also, he smoked. He knew about the seriousness of these conditions and could explain the dire consequences of not caring for oneself to the many patients with whom he shared them.

"Big Bill" I named him, secretly, and it was often to Big Bill I went for an explanation of the longings and needs of addiction, or when I needed a good laugh.

He was a wonderful cook, dreaming up concoctions the would-be chefs on the cooking channels would die for. If hand-cut pasta with black truffle butter was called for, then that was what there would be.

Some nurses were the epitome of high fashion. One, probably middle-aged—although it was hard to tell her age because she always looked wonderful, and never changed over the years—had her color palette done and carried a pile of swatches around with her. Everything matched, from the frames of her many stylish pairs of glasses to her watches. Another nurse, an extremely attractive woman of Filipino and Caucasian heritage, suddenly began to appear for work in stiletto heels and revealing, low-cut dresses. How she walked through muddy gardens and potholes without twisting an ankle was astonishing to me, although she surely aerated the soil. Her once lovely figure began dwindling away before our eyes, and we became concerned she was anorexic. One morning over coffee she tearily confessed to having discovered her husband was cheating on her with his younger secretary. Once they worked things out she regained her curves and dressed in a manner more appropriate for visiting patients, many of whom were young men. Her previously cheery, take-charge demeanor returned.

The nursing supervisor, a large woman who shuffled along without lifting her feet and was not in the best of health, made out-of-this-world ice cream—vanilla, coffee, mango, raspberry. Whatever flavor we requested, she produced.

Cooking and baking served as a creative outlet for many of the workers, so we enjoyed potlucks, and there was always a reason for one, from birthdays to holidays to staff meetings. These were our only times to relax, gossip, and gorge ourselves silly. In fact, for a staff of people working in health, we were not the best representatives. Many workers were, like many of our patients, on the verge of being morbidly obese. They smoked, drank endless pots of coffee and sodas, and certainly did not exercise, unless slouching to one's car in a parking lot is considered cardio exercise. I remembered that in the hospitals in Israel it was the same. The health workers smoked, ate starchy, greasy cafeteria food, and did not take care of themselves. That is why I became interested in alternative medicine. For me, exercise was a wonderful way to release stress at the end of the day, as were my yoga classes, which I attended as faithfully every Sunday as others attended church.

Of course, the office had to have clerks to handle the paperwork we filled out in triplicate. They typed up requests, sent them out, and kept files on the patients. One of the clerks ambled about at the dazzling pace of a banana slug. She was a large woman whose posture worried me, because her spine curved back and around so that she resembled a question mark which could, at any moment, break in two. She had never missed an episode of *Days of our Lives,* taping it to watch after she went home. Her husband, who sometimes came by to drop off his delicious roast turkey, was slight. They resembled Jack Sprat and his wife. After twenty-five years of marriage, he upped and left her for her best friend, but only after she had caught them in flagrante delicto.

Another clerk, young and vivacious, regularly appeared at the office with deep blue bruises on her arms and wrists, the result of her struggles with her latest boyfriend. She had four children, all fathered by different men. Apparently each man had abused her, but she kept finding the same type. Another clerk was the single mother of two children. Recently she had begun dating again, and was soon to remarry. She planned her upcoming marriage by poring over bridal magazines, with daily input from all of us.

Food and sex, what else is life about? The receptionist received the public in teetering high heels, skintight miniskirts, low-cut tops, and tight chokers fastened around her neck. Her nails, so long they curved downward, were painted with deep red polish that matched her lipstick. No matter the topic—a flu epidemic, movies, children, immigrants, politics, fashion—she always steered the conversation around to sex. One day she and I went for lunch. We sat sipping Diet Coke in a small, crowded burger joint. As we waited for our burgers she announced, in a loud stage whisper, that she had been to a sex shop a few days before because she'd heard a nurse telling a woman who had never experienced an orgasm to buy a vibrator.

"Bless that nurse," she said to me, still in a loud whisper. "I drove straight there after work, and there was a whole wall of these things. A whole wall," she repeated, holding her hands out wide. "I searched until I found what looked like the perfect one, and I bought it. I have named it, and I keep it under my bed and worship it," she said, putting her hands together and rolling her eyes heavenward, as if praying. "It is my new saint."

CHAPTER 12

I have many friends and family members from South Africa and Israel who have settled here and seem to have assimilated quite comfortably. I did not find this transition easy; I always feel as if I am experiencing life from the outside. Of course, when I am around Americans, which is most of the time, my accent doesn't help. Immediately I open my mouth, people are aware that I am different.

I went to evaluate an elderly white gentleman who lived in Martinez. The nurse had already assigned a home health aide to bathe him. I met the aide, a white woman, at his home so that I could give her the necessary instructions.

I could not understand why the man was so rude to me after initially allowing me into his home. No matter what I said or did, he snapped at me, making it quite clear I was not welcome. On the other hand, he was genial and polite to the aide. Afterward, as we walked to our cars, I asked her what I had done wrong.

"Nothing at all," she said, "but you have an accent, you are a foreigner. He hates foreigners."

I speak English, not American. Soon after I began work, it became apparent that what I said was unintelligible to a vast number of people, even though I tried my best to modify my accent and choice of words. I labeled many patients as having receptive aphasia, which means they have lost their ability to understand language.

One day I told an African American woman I would see her on the fifth.

"The first?" she asked.

"No, the fifth."

"Okay then, Monday."

"No, Friday the fifth."

This was getting nowhere. I had not realized how obviously addled this poor woman was. I tried again.

"Okay Millie, I be seeing you on the feefth."

"That's good, sugar," she said, lying in her bed. "I hear you. I'll look out for you Friday, then."

Now, years later, when I hear "I have to axe someone" I no longer think someone is about to be chopped into pieces. I sometimes say "feefth" for fifth, "awerenge" for orange, "your legs look all swole up," or "I'll be seein' you real soon."

At these times the spirit of my high school English teacher, cane in hand, looms above me. In his crisp, precisely enunciated English, he says, "Nesta, Nesta, is this what we worked for all those years?"

In South Africa my home language was English, but we had to learn Afrikaans, the most official language of South Africa, from first grade. I studied French in high school. My parents used a spattering of Yiddish with my grandparents so that we, the children, would not understand. Of course we quickly learned the gist of what they were saying. Also, we were constantly surrounded by the rich tapestry of sounds of the Africans who worked in our home.

Only once during the years of working in home health did I have an opportunity to try Yiddish. A nurse asked me to assist with an old couple, recent immigrants from Russia. I explained to her that my Yiddish was extremely limited, if not downright nonexistent, but she insisted because she only spoke English. The sour smell of boiled cabbage and onion permeated the passageway well before we reached their apartment. An old woman with a scarf wrapped around her head opened the door, peeked out, then let us in. Her husband was quite obviously beyond talking in any language. Corpselike, he lay on the bed, covered with khaki blankets. The whitest toes I had ever seen stuck out from underneath the pile. His wife seemed to be raving, speaking Russian in loud bursts and then flapping her hands. Between rants she placed her hands to her temples and squeezed them, as if to keep her head from bursting. The nurse and I looked at each other helplessly until I heard the woman say something like *"ich hobbe mir a cholem."* I understood she was trying to convey that she was having a nightmare, and it dawned upon me that she, and not her obviously very ill husband, needed help. Goodness knows how I managed to ask her whether she was having a nightmare or a bad dream, in my strange mixture of German, Yiddish, and Afrikaans, but she understood my question and told me she'd had a terrible headache, so she'd helped herself to her husband's pills, and now her head was reeling, she was seeing things, and she was petrified she would die alongside of him. I relayed this to the nurse.

"She did what?" asked the nurse. "Which of his pills?"

The woman pointed to one of the many bottles standing on a shelf.

"Oh my goodness," said the nurse. "That is her husband's morphine! How many did she take?"

Thank goodness everything turned out all right. After a cup of tea the woman calmed down, and I explained to her, in my strange mixture of languages, that she couldn't just help herself to her husband's medicine: a pill is not a magic cure-all.

Besides the above-mentioned polyglot, I speak and read Hebrew—a lot of languages, yes, but all totally useless in Contra Costa County. I began listening to Spanish language cassettes in my car, as well as to the various Spanish radio stations, but I balked at Vietnamese, Cambodian, Tagalog, Mandarin, Cantonese, Mien, Khmu, Hindi, Russian, Urdu, and Farsi. Enough is enough. When I first began working, we used interpreters. Later, when the budget cuts began, these and other essential services were eliminated, and we resorted to pantomime, sometimes with tragic results. I felt as if I were playing charades, but no one could guess the name of the book.

CHAPTER 13

Very soon I learned that, besides being an occupational therapist, I would become a counselor, a mediator, a social worker, a
home decorator, a sympathetic friend. I came into contact with
and learned about cultures I had never before encountered. Any
knowledge I gleaned was from questioning the interpreters and
the families themselves, and reading as many articles and books
as I could lay my hands on. Most of my coworkers wanted to
get in and out of homes as quickly as possible; they were not
interested in the backgrounds of the patients. But it was because
I asked questions of my patients and listened to their answers
that I became privy to all sorts of information and fascinating
stories. Everyone I had the privilege of meeting had a story, and
often I asked if I could write about them. The reply was always
one of delight. A Mien woman, whose words were translated by
her daughter, told me that "in the way of our people and those
who came before us, my family want their story to be known.
You have my blessings."

The interpreters shared our office space. In Concord there
were interpreters of Arabic, Afghani, and Russian languages. In
the Richmond office were many Asian language interpreters.
Over the years we got to know each other, and we shared the
ongoing events of our lives. The Asian interpreters, who spoke
Mien, Hmong, Khmu, Vietnamese, Mandarin, and Cantonese,
always brought their lunch with them and ate in the workers'
lunchroom. Many a time I sat with them, lured by tantalizing
smells of garlic, curry, hot chilies, sesame, and soy. Every day
they ate the type of food I only ate in restaurants. In general
these women seemed sweet, polite, and shy, maybe because
of their culture, or maybe because of their difficulties with the

English language and a new way of life in which women had more say than they had known previously.

I developed a love of pho, especially in winter. Pho is a large, steaming pot of broth in which simmer pieces of crab, fish cake, mussels, and other seafood, with either rice or egg noodles. Or it can be made with slices of pork, beef, and chicken, tendon and tripe, brisket, bean sprouts, basil, cilantro (horrors, this I fastidiously remove), and on the side, limes, thai basil, and various spices like oyster sauce and hot chili oil. I saw a recipe for this one day in the food section of the *San Francisco Chronicle*. That day at lunch I told six Asian workers that I found a recipe for pho, pronouncing it as "foe." Twelve eyes looked at me quizzically. "You know," I said, "that delicious soup, the one that comes in big bowls—a meal unto itself—'foe.'" After much more explanation and description on my part, six mouths in unison pronounced it in different ways: "Foa, fa, fe, faeh," etc. Thank goodness they were too polite to burst into uncontrolled laughter at my mispronunciation.

Almost all of them, as sweet and unassuming as they appeared, had fled dreadful wars, survived refugee camps, and come to America, where they studied English, found jobs, and supported families. One day a Mien woman, who looked like a teenager but had daughters sixteen and eighteen years old, told me the story of how she fled Laos (or "Low," as they pronounce it) with her parents. For three months they climbed over mountains, surviving on grass, grubs, and worms—when they were lucky enough to find any. Sometimes planes flew overhead and strafed them. I remembered the spine-tingling wail of the air raid sirens during the Yom Kippur War, then the rush of adrenaline as we fled to the shelters. They did not have sirens to warn them, and they did not have shelters to run to: instead they threw themselves down on the ground and hoped to avoid the strafing. She married in the refugee camp and, together with her husband and parents, settled in Oakland and raised a family. Not long after she told me this we had lunch together. She told me how, two weeks before, she and her husband had gone to see friends in Oakland. He got out of the car after her and locked it. She had already begun walking when she heard a scuffling sound and turned back to see two men accosting her husband. Luckily, all they did was grab his watch, because she said she was so frightened she did not turn back to help him, but instead fled in a panic to their friends' home.

Although their culture is so different from anything I know, I nevertheless feel a strong affinity with these refugees from Asia and Southeast Asia. Like so many Jews, they fled persecution and wars and came here to start a new life. We share values, such as the importance of family and education. I remember my father always saying, "Anyone can take everything from you, but not what you have in your head." We, like them, keep our traditions and history alive and pass them on to the next generation. Fleeing pogroms and poverty, my grandparents went to South Africa from Lithuania. Within one generation, our family was South African in mannerisms and speech, albeit Jewish South African. However, because of my grandparents, especially my maternal grandmother, and their stories, my heritage always remained vividly alive and formed as much of my psyche as if I had lived through these events myself: working as peasant farmers for feudal land barons, surviving pogroms and persecution, fleeing to search for a new, more hospitable land, struggling to assimilate in totally foreign countries and cultures.

. . .

"How did you get to this country?" I asked a Vietnamese man, a chemical engineer who had taken leave from work to care for his ailing father-in-law.

"I fled Vietnam on a raft, together with at least forty other people. Thai pirates robbed us of our food and the few possessions we had. Fourteen days we drifted without food or drink. We became desperate. Some people went crazy from the thirst, drinking seawater, even their own urine. We rolled the dead bodies overboard. After fourteen days a large tanker picked us up. The tanker belonged to Chevron. I work for them now."

This flight took place fourteen years before. Now he and his Vietnamese wife own a large home with a view of San Pablo Bay. His wife has a manicure salon. They converse with their two young children in Vietnamese. On Sunday their children attend a special school where they learn about the history and culture of Vietnam. They send money to their family left behind in Vietnam.

In their garden a wooden bridge arches over a pond in which fat koi move lazily. Next to the pond, at the foot of the bridge, a statue of a smiling Buddha raises his arms toward heaven.

Many of the Asian refugees settled in Richmond and San Pablo. In western Contra Costa County, the largest populations are Laotian and Mien, but there are also Khmu, Hmong, and Khmer. They each speak their own language and don't particularly like or trust each other, although in America they are learning to mix. These people were recruited by the CIA to battle the Vietcong. In return they were promised assistance and a safe haven in the event they had to leave. When the Vietcong took over Laos, they began slaughtering those who had fought against them. The CIA fled, forgetting their promise of help. This is vividly portrayed in Anne Fadiman's book *The Spirit Catches You and You Fall Down*. She writes about the Hmong community in Merced, who were also recruited by the CIA; the stories of each tribe are similar. From our interpreters, and books published locally by working collectives, I learned there are at least two hundred tribes in the hills and mountains of Laos and Thailand, each with its separate identity, language, beliefs, costumes, and foods. Most of these cultures are preliterate, with a strong oral tradition.

I met these tribal people before Anne Fadiman's book came out, but as soon as I read it, I passed it along to my coworkers, who were having a hard time understanding the behavior of these spirited people. Why did they insist on sitting on low stools after hip replacement surgery? This was against all precautions.

Why did they hang their clothing on the bedside commodes we ordered for them and place TVs on the tub transfer benches? Big Bill read the book overnight, then passed it on.

How these hardy people have survived in America is a mystery to me. It took English-speaking, Western-raised me years to begin to accommodate to a new way of life and learn an entirely different set of customs, and I came with an education and knowledge of places other than my immediate birthplace.

In their country of lofty peaks and steep ravines, the Mien did not have electricity. They chopped wood and used it to cook and heat their homes. They killed their pigs, chickens, and deer, fished, and grew their own vegetables. The words for "supermarket," "bank," "laundromat," "mall," "cinema," or just about anything else Americans take for granted were not in their vocabulary.

Like all immigrants, they struggle to learn a new language and baffling new customs. In order to apply for immigration status, health benefits, and food stamps, they have to fill in reams of paperwork, a daunting prospect for anyone. Sometimes they presented me with official letters from Medi-Cal or the INS (Immigration and Naturalization Service) and asked me to explain them. I read and reread the letters, but I could not quite decipher what the officials wanted, and I certainly couldn't explain it.

. . .

The sheet I held in my hand stated that a man of Laotian origin, eighty years old, had suffered a stroke leaving his entire left side paralyzed. He and his wife lived with their daughter and her family in subsidized housing in Richmond.

I climbed the concrete steps to the second floor of the nondescript apartment building, which surrounded a dusty courtyard. In the middle of the yard tomato plants, tied to poles, flourished in a tiny patch of cultivated earth. Squash, mint, and parsley surrounded the tomatoes. Latino and Asian faces peered at me from behind window bars. I knocked on the door of a second-floor apartment. A young woman with black hair wound into a knot, wearing a long orange, white, and black batik print skirt wrapped around her waist, let me in. The living room consisted of about four low, round, straw stools, an old sofa whose springs had given up, and a TV. The pictures on the TV were fuzzy and the voices coming out of the set crackled. A few books were scattered on a shelf alongside photographs of people in elaborately embroidered clothing grouped closely together in front of high mountains. A vaguely grassy smell of steamed white rice filled the space.

The woman, who told me her name was Lai, which means last child, showed me into the bedroom. Two people lay on a mattress. A tiny, dark-skinned man, although naked from the waist up, looked clothed because his entire body was covered in intricate blue tattoos of an abstract design—a human batik. His wife wore a scarf tied around her head and a batik skirt like that of her daughter. The old man awoke, sat up, put his hands together in front of his heart, and bowed to me. I bowed back, pleased to see he could still manage this gesture of greeting; it boded well for his prognosis. In other words, he knew that I, a stranger, had come to see him. That he could put his hands together at midline meant he had return of movement, and also he had no left-side neglect. My observation skills were such an essential part of my work that I always took in everything from the moment I opened my car door. His eyes gleamed, bright, intelligent, and vital. His wife sat up, groaning, as she adjusted her headscarf and clutched her lower back.

Their daughter translated. I asked her what her parents did before coming to America. She told me they had been rice farmers. The tattoos, she said, are a sign of bravery; if one can handle being tattooed, it means one can withstand pain. When the Vietcong took over in 1975, their family of eight fled their village to make the perilous crossing over the Mekong River into Thailand. During their flight, one of their sons was killed by the Communists. They had no time to mourn but continued running, surviving on grass, insects, and plants. In Thailand they were placed in a refugee camp. The daughter said that the camp was no refuge. "One morning my father was punished because he didn't know he had to salute the Thai flag. The Thais beat him and put him in jail for two weeks."

After a few years their papers were processed, and now they live in Richmond, California, about as far removed from the mountains of Laos as heaven is from earth.

The old man had not lost his fighting spirit. As bravely as he must have fended for his family, undergone being tattooed, fought in the war, and begun the long journey to America, so did he work at regaining the strength of his affected side. He faithfully followed his exercises and made a swift recovery. His wife also told me she needed help, her back hurt. It looked like it must, because every time I saw her she was clutching her lower back. She pulled down her shirt and showed me burn marks down her sternum. These were not ordinary marks: it looked like someone had stamped her symmetrically along either side of her sternum with a red marker. The daughter told me a Laotian healer had tried to rid her of her back pain by placing burning pieces of bamboo on her. It sounded like the stories I had heard in Israel about the *beigelmacher* (a big-shot baker of bagels). He was a well-known healer from Eastern Europe. During the week he worked as a baker (hence "beigelmacher," and also because he used his hands to knead dough). On Saturdays, lines of people from all over the country waited to be kneaded by his healing hands. Sometimes he placed hot cups on aching muscles to draw out the toxins.

I subsequently saw marks similar to this woman's red dots on other patients. Unfortunately, without a referral I was not allowed to work with her. I explained this to the daughter but did suggest some exercises for her mother to help alleviate the pain.

During my visits, the daughter sat with us to translate, and she told me some of their beliefs and traditions.

"Food is an important part of our culture," she said. "We eat special foods when someone is sick. When a woman is pregnant she eats soups to keep her and the baby strong. There are dishes for the New Year, for weddings, and funerals.

"We eat food to prevent menstrual cramps, to aid childbirth, to calm the nerves and the stomach.

"It is fall now, and soon flu season begins. Next time you come I will make something to keep you strong during winter. You will not get colds or flu easily. We grow herbs in our garden to make the food. The seeds are sent from our family in the camps in Thailand."

The next visit, she invited me into the kitchen. In front of her, on a chopping board, lay a green pepper and two red peppers of the long, thin, extremely spicy variety. She placed leaves and flowers from their garden on the chopping board together with slices of ginger root. Three eggs sat in a bowl nearby, ready to be used. She chopped the vegetables into tiny pieces. The blade flew. After a few seconds she stopped, looked at her work, and declared that she must chop some more. When the vegetables resembled grains of sand on a beach, she cracked the eggs into a dish one at a time, to ensure they were fresh, and placed them in a ceramic bowl, beating them together. She then folded the infinitesimal vegetables into the egg mixture, covered the bowl with foil, and carefully placed it into a large pot of boiling water. She put a lid on the pot, allowing the mixture to steam.

When the omelet was ready she removed the lid, allowing the steam to escape. She placed towels around her hands, lifted out the dish, and turned it over onto a serving plate. A perfect, dome-shaped omelet appeared, spongy and glittering with the chopped ingredients. We ate it before it cooled. She and her parents smacked their lips loudly. After a few mouthfuls I became aware that my heart was beating faster and my face felt flushed. A luxuriant heat welled up inside of me.

That winter I did not get sick.

On my last visit, the man and his wife squatted on the low straw stools in the living room, chewing leaves sent from relatives in Laos. They spat long streams of brown juice into small silver bowls on the floor next to the stools. Through his daughter, I told him he had progressed really well, and I no longer needed to return. He put his hands together in the traditional greeting, bowed, then waved a cheery good-bye with his left hand.

CHAPTER 14

To become old, debilitated, and unwanted is a frightening prospect. Somehow it seems worse in America, because the old are tossed aside. At least in Asian cultures elders are cared for and respected for their wisdom, experience, and the knowledge which they have accumulated. After seeing people leave their homes for skilled nursing facilities or boarding homes, I feel frightened for my future. What if I age without any money? Will my retirement savings become worthless? Will I have no family to care for me? What if I become demented? What if I lose my independence? I remember distinctly two women with whom I worked in a skilled nursing facility. One had Alzheimer's and must have come from money, because she was always surrounded by a coterie of attentive caregivers. Every time I popped in to see her, she commented on my curls, or my rings. She gazed at my hair with childlike, clear blue eyes, then lifted a hand to reach out and play with my curls. She always wore a blue sapphire ring, which matched the blue of her eyes, surrounded by small diamonds. Her lustrous white hair was impeccably washed, curled, and lacquered, and she was tastefully attired. Like the queen of England, she always carried a purse in her lap or over her arm. One day at lunch in the communal dining hall she looked in my direction and crooked her forefinger, beckoning me over. I went to her. She dabbed at her lips with her napkin, leaned toward me and whispered, "This is really embarrassing. How will I pay for this meal?"

I assured her she didn't have to pay, but she became so agitated and concerned that quite soon she had to be led back to her room.

The other woman, a charming lady from Norway, fainted in the therapy room. I cradled her head in my lap as she repeated, "I need air." I took her to an open window, sat her in a chair, and fanned her. Then she said, "I need air in my room, but how can I afford a room with a bed by the window?"

How awful, I thought, to become ill with the thought of money on one's mind.

On the other hand, early one morning I walked into the room of an ancient black woman who shared the room with two other patients. I had never seen anyone come to visit her, and she had no visible means of support.

"Hallelujah," came a voice from the tiny withered figure as I approached her bed. "Hallelujah, honey," she beamed toothlessly in my direction, raising her arms and waving. "Yet another beautiful day, blessed be." She praised me, praised her accommodations, and praised the food she had just finished eating. The whole of her emaciated, crooked little being radiated genuine delight with her lot in life.

In the same home I was delighted to discover a ninety-four-year-old South African woman, a long-retired headmistress who was a resident in the facility. She too had no family, and probably most of the people she knew were long dead. Her mind was still astonishingly sharp, and though her body was falling apart, organ by organ, joint by joint, she never complained and always appeared content. One day I walked in to find her lying, quite happy, on the floor next to her bed. I hurried over and bent down to help her stand. When, finally, after many creaks and grunts, she collapsed back on the bed, she said to me, "Oh, you sure missed the fun, seeing me roll off the bed. Quite amusing, my dear."

Of course there are old and discarded Asians in America, and there are also outstanding senior centers for Asians, but I did not come across Asians in residential homes very often. Almost always, the younger generation cares for the older generation in their own home. I remember one case that vaguely resembled that of a family member being "put away."

Tree Barking

The nurse, physical therapist, speech therapist, and I were
sent to the home of a woman in her mid-sixties who suffered
from high blood pressure and diabetes. Several years before,
she'd had a stroke that left her right side contracted and paralyzed. Recently she'd suffered yet another stroke, which rendered her aphasic (unable to speak) and weak on her left side.

She and her husband lived in a pleasant home in San Pablo.
The first time I went, a good-looking man in his mid-thirties
opened the door and introduced himself as the son. He was tall,
with light-colored skin, thick black hair, and Asian-looking blue
eyes. His mom was Japanese. She and her husband met during
the Second World War when he served in the U.S. Navy and was
stationed in Japan. They fell in love, married in Japan, and then
after the war settled in San Pablo. They raised two children, who
were both present on my visit.

Their mother sat on a wheelchair in the living room, a nice-
looking woman despite the strokes. She had smooth skin and
thick black hair. Her lips slanted upward into a smile on the right
side of her face; the left side could not move. Something about
her demeanor reminded me of films or TV shows I had seen
about samurai: she emanated a sense of pride, of being able to
challenge something huge. She approached her disabilities with
this determination, following through with our instructions.

The living room bore evidence of their life in Japan. Silk
kimono prints on the walls were tastefully displayed, alongside
fans and swords. In the dining room, potted plants with shining
leaves were surrounded by warrior dolls that reflected the proud
demeanor of the woman.

For good reason, she was extremely frustrated and upset by
her present condition. Her husband was apparently completely
devoted to her and attended to her every need. However, he
had collapsed the night before, and their children had taken him
to the hospital, where he was kept for observation. Until he
returned home, the children were caring for her.

Several months later, after we'd discharged her, we learned
to our dismay that she'd had to undergo a radical mastectomy,

after which she suffered yet another stroke. While she was in the hospital recovering from the mastectomy, her husband died. We wrote to the family expressing our sympathy, which was indeed heartfelt.

A year later, I walked down the corridor toward the exit of a sparsely furnished board and care home. The residents were lined up along the walls in their wheelchairs, waiting for the dining room doors to open. Suddenly I thought I recognized the samurai, slumped over in a wheelchair. Her hair was gray, dry, and sparse, and patches of scalp showed through. I went up to her and put my arm around her. "Yes," she remembered me. In a whisper she said, "Everything gone, all at the same time, my husband, my breast, my home."

CHAPTER 15

Like everything else in life, referrals came in cycles; similar diseases, similar circumstances. There was a while when we were sent, quite frequently, to homes to evaluate parents who had come from overseas to visit their children in America. Either on the flight, or after being here a couple of weeks, one of them had suffered a major stroke

This time I was on my way to see a man from the Philippines. He and his wife had been visiting their daughter, a nurse, when he suffered a stroke. Luckily, his daughter knew how to get appropriate help, and he was now recovering.

On my first visit, two girls, two and four years old, greeted me at the door. They grinned, peering up at me from under long, black lashes. I looked down at two shiny heads of straight, glossy, thick, black hair. While I spoke to the father, the girls inspected me. On my next visit they were looking for me out of the window. Gleefully they called out my name, then raced to let me in. While I was busy with the father, the little one poked me. I turned around to see what she wanted. She held out her two little fists, then opened them. In both hands were mung beans. She put her hands behind her back, then brought them back out and opened them again. Magically, only one hand contained the beans. Throughout this performance her older sister continued her scrutiny of me. Suddenly she said, in a serious tone, "You have a very long nose."

She held out the thumb and forefinger of her left hand so I could see just how long. She made the space between her fingers even wider, "very long."

Mortified, I told the physical therapist about this when I returned to the office. She is Chinese, and she laughed heartily when I told her the story, which I didn't consider the least bit funny.

"They have never been out of their home," she said, chuckling. "Just what kind of noses do you think they have seen?"

"Well," I replied, "it sure touched a nerve in me."

In the closely knit Jewish world in which I grew up, long noses were certainly not regarded as a banner of pride. I spent my school years with a pencil pushed under my nose, praying the tip would move skyward. Those long-term persistent efforts had absolutely no effect. By the time I turned sixteen, many of my contemporaries had "had their noses done." The most desired nose was the one delicately carved by Dr. Penn to honor, I think, his wife's lovely nose. It was easy to spot a Dr. Penn nose: they were straight and slender and the tip curved delicately upward, leaving no trace of offensive Semitic heritage. I would have loved such a nose, but my parents would not listen to my pleas, and these curious little girls graphically reminded me of my suppressed desire.

CHAPTER 16

Every day is new and different. On a daily basis I encounter racism, classism, love, and acceptance. I am forced to face my own prejudices and biases, and I certainly do not like many of the things I encounter in myself, especially when, far too often, I find myself sitting in judgment. Goodness knows I've struggled to keep my mind as open and unsullied as I know how, but learning to suspend judgment has been extremely difficult, especially when I've had to endure the careless judgment of others.

In the dining room of an elderly Caucasian couple in Concord, I sit face-to-face with the husband of a demented old woman who, along with a host of other illnesses, has recently suffered a debilitating stroke. The room smells strongly of urine. The woman is incontinent and she has been sitting in her diaper for quite some time. She is very thin and her flesh sags down her body, bare except for the soggy diaper. She lists to her right and there is a deep red and blue bruise on her left arm. The man has red-rimmed, small, blue eyes surrounded by sparse, sandy lashes. A rifle is slung across a chair in the corner. He tells me that the "China woman hurt my wife's arm." He must be referring to the physical therapist, who is as American as apple pie but of Chinese ancestry. She would never hurt anyone. Before I can say anything, he adds that this morning a "colored lady" arrived and said she was here to bathe his wife. "I didn't let her in," he tells me, with something akin to pride.

What a pity, I think. She would have comforted your wife. Everyone else wants her to come on a daily, if not hourly, basis. And now you have the Jew lady in your home. Isn't it strange that those you shun are the ones who have come to help?

I don't say this aloud. It would be unprofessional, and there is a rifle close by.

Another time, I am sitting in a house in Pittsburg. An old man has fallen several times while bathing. I am here to assess the situation. He sits in a chair while his daughter-in-law stands close by, ready to do his bidding. He is not exactly cooperative: he kind of grunts in answer to questions, and she elaborates. While we talk we hear the mail being delivered through the slot. "Bring it here," he says, and she does so. A pamphlet is among the bills. "Israel Education Day" is written on it in white letters.

"What's this?" He picks it up. "What the hell is this? Who sent this to us? I want nothing to do with those people. What do they think we want to know about them folks? Education? Crap. Just keep them away from here."

I listen in silence. His daughter-in-law appears flustered and apologetic, even though she has no idea of my background. When she walks me to my car, she tells me that when she had accompanied him to the doctor's office yesterday, he had spoken loudly about the Black and Latino people in the waiting room. He didn't want to sit near them. His daughter-in-law is Japanese.

For the first time in my life, I found that I barely finished introducing myself before letting people know I am Jewish. I would either say I was Jewish, or in the course of conversation I would mention that I had lived in Israel, and hope they had heard of the country. This was a preventive measure, to save people from saying something stupid, like "I was in South Africa when I was in the Navy and I saw people breaking into Jew-owned businesses. All the Jews there work in diamonds." A man once told me this. It was certainly news to me.

When I lived in Israel, the entire population was certain that our tiny, troubled little country was the center of the world. It was inconceivable to us, unimaginable in fact, that there were people on the planet who had not heard of our country. Unfortunately, we always seemed to be at the epicenter of whatever war, outbreak of hostilities, or terrorist activity was going on in the Middle East, if not the world. To my amazement, when

I came here I discovered that many people have never heard of Israel. The concept of the Middle East is unclear, and I find people lump Iranians, Iraqis, Afghanis, Israelis, and Palestinians together—somewhere in the world outside of America. Indeed, to keep track of the groups, countergroups, different sects, and so on is more than confusing, especially for people whose knowledge of geography is poor. There are people born in the East Bay who have never been to San Francisco. What is stranger is that they don't even want to visit San Francisco, let alone other parts of the country, not to mention the world.

A new group of people for me was "white trash." The men, often covered in crude, blue-ink tattoos received in jail, smoke and drink unabashedly, unaware of the bans on smoking not too far from where they reside. They drink pots of coffee with sugar in it, along with beer. They don't appear to work; they sit on old lumpy sofas, beer cans in hand, looking at Jerry Springer on TV, or the various "Judge" shows. Old cars and piles of junk, like broken washing machines and refrigerators, are strewn on the areas in front of the homes (I hesitate to use the word "lawns"). They own pit bulls and Rottweilers. A bearded, tattooed man, cigarette in one hand, his other on his pit bull's collar, assured me that the dog was well trained and friendly. Dragging on his cigarette, he also told me that when his mom had fallen in the shower two days before, he'd called the paramedics and they made him take the dog outside before they would enter the house.

This group didn't appear to care for people of color, gays, in fact anyone different from them, and didn't care who knew. These people were so politically incorrect that I found them refreshing.

The aides, some nurses, the other therapist, and I tried to get together at least once a month for happy hour. Over a margarita or a well drink it was a pleasure to tell stories, laugh, and gossip. One night at such a gathering, I confessed how surprised I was about meeting "white trash," who seem so ignorant and judgmental of others. A black nurse listened, then nodded sympathetically. She dipped a tortilla chip into salsa and confessed that she had a hard time with "black trash," whom she found to be remarkably similar.

At one point I received a slew of referrals to yet another subculture, long-distance truck drivers who had undergone heart attacks. After a few visits I was able to predict what I would find: a Confederate flag on a wall, empty Jack Daniels bottles on tables, Cokes and Coors and Miller beer cans scattered over beds and floors. In bed a youngish (mid-thirties, early forties) truck driver, often alongside a younger (late twenties) female. Usually the woman is coming off some kind of drug as she shivers and sniffs, while her eyes, with pupils the size of either pinpoints or craters, water. Twenty-dollar bills are strewn around like discarded Kleenex.

It makes me nervous to know that these are the very people barreling behind me on the freeway, flicking their headlights and honking when I am apparently not moving fast enough for them. Now when I see a big rig in my rear view mirror, I swiftly move to the furthest lane possible.

One truck driver I found alone in bed surrounded by personals torn from the local paper. He showed me his personal ad: "an ugly frog looking for a princess." I thought that was a remarkably apt description. On my last visit I found him listening to the news when I walked in.

"Can you believe it?" he asked as soon as I entered. "See what women make men do? Can you believe they're going to take O. J. in for the murder of his wife?"

I had no idea whom or what he was talking about, but by the end of that day, after at least three more patients had spoken about O. J., I knew I should know who this was. Embarrassed by my ignorance, I never asked any of them, just nodding in concern and surprise with each patient. In my car I listened to the news of O. J. Simpson, which was on every station. I returned to the office, and to the collective disbelief of my workers, confessed that I had no idea who this person was. I was immediately enlightened.

CHAPTER 17

Many times I received referrals I thought I simply could not handle. Working in home health is not the same as working in a rehabilitation center or in a hospital with, say, stroke patients, or people suffering from traumatic brain injury. In these settings the treatment is routine and predictable. In the home environment every situation is new and challenging, and there were many times I felt I was simply incapable of doing good work. The cases were so complex, and out of the realm of my experience. In fact, for all I knew, I was causing irreparable harm to someone.

One drizzly afternoon I stood at my desk, staring in dismay at the referral.

"Nine-month male achondroplastic dwarf, DD (developmentally delayed), hydrocephalic, oxygen dependent, tracheal tube. Not expected to survive for long. Adopted by dwarf mothers."

These terse statements filled me with horror and dread. With trembling hands I picked up the referral sheets and walked to my supervisor's desk. Displaying a bravado I did not feel, I waved them in her face.

"Please," I begged, "don't do this to me."

"It looks interesting." She smiled encouragingly, and clicked her pen.

"You go and see how interesting it is. I barely know what to do with a normal baby, let alone a deformed infant on oxygen. This one is for Fellini. Please don't make me go."

To no avail. One bright Tuesday morning I found myself staring at a sign on the door: "Welcome friends." This friend breathed deep, knocked, and waited, not knowing what to expect.

A plump, pleasant looking woman of average height opened the door. She had lovely hazel eyes and the corners of her mouth turned upward in a welcoming smile. In her arms she held a tiny body with such a large head that the total effect resembled that of a balloon someone had been unable to finish blowing up. A tube descended into his trachea through a hole in the front of his throat. The woman introduced herself as the nurse and invited me in. The mothers would soon be in, she said.

I entered the living room. Averting my eyes from the creature in her arms, I surveyed the scene. On the wall-to-wall, dark blue carpet lay a white sheet for the infant. Toy cars, an assortment of rubber ducks, teething rings, and plastic blocks were scattered around. More toys were piled into crates. The dining room consisted of a short pine table and chairs. Everything in the house was miniature: the furniture, the cabinets, even the toilet and washbasin. Like Alice in Wonderland, I felt myself growing taller and taller. My neck stretched upward and, like a giraffe, I could make no sounds. I scanned the small world beneath me, sunk onto the floor, and stared again at the creature. He looked somewhat like ET. His head was quite out of proportion to his tiny body. His spinal column showed signs of kyphosis, curving upward like that of the Hunchback of Notre Dame. Rolls of flesh encased his tiny limbs. His eyes met mine and I attempted a smile. His eyes were large and sparkly blue, surrounded by dark lashes. For a moment I wanted to reach out and hold him, but I was afraid, not knowing whether I would have enough strength to support that head, which was covered with fine, straight brown hair. In my still horrified mind's eye I could see it falling off his neck, clunking down onto the carpet, rolling out the front door, down the driveway, gaining momentum as it continued rolling toward the freeway.

As I envisioned this horrendous scene, a tiny woman, about three and a half feet tall, walked in.

"Hi," she smiled. "I'm Carol, Shirley will be here soon."

A couple of minutes later Shirley, an enormous ball with a tiny head, waddled in, breathing heavily. She plopped, belly down, onto the rug and propped herself on her elbows. The three of them chatted and laughed. Within a short while I joined the conversation. The nurse placed ET on the sheet next to me. I placed a toy music box next to his head and banged on it, setting off the tune "Winnie the Pooh." Sam (ET's real name) smiled delightedly.

Carol and Shirley were schoolteachers. Their interesting and full lives were marred by the fact that, because of their dwarfism, they could not bear children. Practicing Pentecostals, they had prayed for a child, and in flew Sam in answer to their prayers.

Their odd shapes vanished as I listened to the story of Sam. He was born to normal parents in their late teens. The father wanted to give him up for adoption. The mother didn't, but apparently, after trying to keep him at home and take care of his medical needs, she became deeply depressed. After a month she called a social worker, who found him dehydrated and close to death. Until these moms adopted him, he'd been in six different families and about as many hospitals. The adoptive mothers were told he wouldn't survive for more than a few weeks, but in their hearts they knew he'd live.

While we spoke he turned the music box on and off with his chin, setting off "Winnie the Pooh." His large head remained on the sheet because he did not have strong enough musculature to support it, but he slid his chin back and forth. He grinned, appearing delighted with his achievement. He looked up at me and smiled again, his eyelashes fluttering, and before I could even think, I had reached out, picked him up, and cradled him in my arms. His head stayed on his neck.

Sam was not developmentally delayed, but he had suffered severe environmental deprivation. He responded to treatment immediately. The physical therapist and I went to their home at least twice a week for almost a year. We focused our treatment on normal development, balance, weight shifting, and self help—for instance, to hold his sippy cup himself. Every visit was a miracle of joy and growth. After about three visits he recognized me, and a radiant grin lit up his face when he saw me walking in. Not too long after that he began raising his chubby little arm, to wave.

Within a month Sam was able to keep his head upright. He learned to hold his bottle. His mothers began taking him to church every Sunday. After his first visit to church, Sam sat in his chair, raised his roly-poly little arms, and waved them back and forth in a fervent "Hallelujah."

The loving and joyful atmosphere drew warm responses from everyone who entered the home: the oxygen delivery man, the postman, other young children who lived in the complex.

There were several times when Sam became ill. His fever rose alarmingly. It was pathetic to see him lying limply, as his tiny chest rose and fell, struggling for air. At times like these, it seemed as if the predictions would come true, and he would die soon. But he always rallied, sometimes to everyone's surprise.

Within about eight months he became feisty. If he didn't want to drink, he pushed his sippy cup away, knocking it off the table. He made a great fuss when he didn't want to wear shoes, kicking his little legs about, making it difficult to dress him. Soon Sam was well enough to leave his home to attend a special school.

Two years after we finished working with him, I spoke to his family. Sam is well. He no longer needs oxygen, and after his tracheal tube was removed and the hole closed, he learned to talk. He also communicates in sign language. Although he cannot walk unassisted, he can walk with a walker, and he also has a wheelchair, which he navigates himself. Sam is happy and doing well in school.

I feel honored to have been part of his development. Moreover, because of Sam and his family I entered a new world of "little people." I realized how our world does not take otherness into account. I can no longer walk into a bank, library, post office, or a supermarket without thinking of them and their constant struggle to see people over a counter, to take objects off shelves, all the things we never ever think about.

Now, whenever I see a little person I smile inwardly, remembering Sam and his warm and wonderful little family.

CHAPTER 18

The first time I went to North Richmond, an area literally on "the other side of the tracks," was one hot summer morning when I still worked out of the Concord office. Most of the workers had definite opinions of Richmond, especially North Richmond. "Don't go there, it's dangerous." "Rather you than me." "I won't go there unless I absolutely have to." My understanding was that if I did go, I would be lucky to get out. If my car and I remained intact, I would be super lucky.

From Martinez I followed Highway 4 west as it wound between rolling hills until it rejoined the I-80 freeway. I exited at Hilltop Drive and drove down to San Pablo Avenue, turning left and then right, onto 23rd Avenue. On the right-hand corner of 23rd and Market was a small shopping center featuring a Mercado Latino selling meat and produce. Next to it was El Yerberito, a shop for herbs and aphrodisiacs from Central and South America: "Make blood strong like bull." There was a laundry, a Salvadorean taqueria, a donut shop, and a liquor store situated alongside a Thai restaurant. I headed west, toward the bay. After I crossed the railroad tracks, the potholes in the road deepened. My Toyota bounced along the rutted road. I drove past a corner store. Outside, black youths wearing oversize, hooded sweatshirts over baggy jeans milled around a graffiti-covered pay phone. I passed a dilapidated building, Temple of Deliverance, before reaching my destination, a small white house with blue trim and a tiny yard featuring dusty, faded rosebushes. A man, his back to me, worked on a car in the driveway next door. Diagonally across the road, the sign on a run-down building proclaimed it to be the Macedonia Missionary Baptist Church. A skinny man sat on the top step. The streetlights, I noticed, were shattered. I did not want to be there when night fell. Sheets of plywood covered the windows of houses that stood in small plots of weeds and grass. Signs on the boards declared these residences out of bounds.

I knocked on the wrought iron protecting the front door and heard someone shout, "Just a minute." After a short while an elderly woman opened the door. She was slightly stooped and walked with the aid of a cane. Her left arm hung loosely at her side as she limped toward me, a result of her recent stroke.

Despite her condition, she cheerfully greeted me, showing me in and gesturing to me to sit next to a table in the entrance. The table was covered by a lace cloth underneath transparent plastic. In the center was a dusty silk flower arrangement, and we peered at each other around the flowers. The kitchen, directly behind the living room, seemed to aspire to minimalism, a gas burner with a stainless steel pot on top of it, and next to that, a small fridge. A clean plate and cup stood on the counter close to the sink.

I walked with her to the bedroom and asked whether she had difficulty getting in and out of the queen-sized bed, which took up almost the entire room.

"No, honey, look how I gets on." So saying, she sat on the edge of the bed, swung her legs around, and lay down. "If I need to, I rolls onto the floor at night. I'm doin' fine."

I gazed at her in astonishment. "Why roll to the floor?"

She looked up toward the ceiling. I followed her gaze and saw bullet holes in the walls. They reminded me of the bullet-marked walls in Jerusalem that surrounded the area known as no-man's-land prior to the Six Day War. But America was not at war.

"What are those from?" I asked.

She limped to the window and said, "See that man, working on the car? He's a crack dealer. I sees him dig a deep hole in his yard, him and another man. They puts the drugs down there and cover them with dirt so's the poh-lice dogs can't smell them.

That place there, over the road," she said, pointing to where the young man sat, "that's a crack house."

"My grandkids are on crack. I told them they are no longer welcome here, but how can I stop them, honey? I'se an old woman. There's no respect for elders no more. Crack cocaine was invented by the devil hisself. You can buy that stuff for one dollar, and folks steal whatever they can lay their hands on for that dollar. I don't have much, honey, but they took my plates, knives and forks, they even stole my bedside commode."

"Don't you call the police?"

She laughed. "The poh-lice don't be comin' here, honey. When the shootin' starts I just rolls on the floor—them bullets don't have eyes."

What could I do but get back to the reason I had come, to help her regain the use of her arm and hand? I showed her exercises to return range of motion back to her affected arm. I also gave her medium-strength therapy putty for fine motor work. This is a plasticine-like material without the smell, graded weak, medium, and strong, depending on the strength of the person to be using it. On our next visit I sat with her as she fashioned farm and domestic animals out of the putty. I asked her whether this area had always been like this.

"No, honey, it was real nice until them addicts and dealers moved in. The sheriffs close one house and a new lot of dealers take over. I'se scared."

I drove back to North Oakland, passing the same corner store with the graffiti-covered pay phone outside. Well out of North Richmond, on San Pablo Avenue, I saw a Safeway and a Lucky store, banks, gas stations; all the amenities we take for granted. A bumper sticker proclaimed, "Free Tibet." I drove through Berkeley, where every second store boasts coffee from far-flung areas of the world: Celebes from Sulawesi, Kona from Hawaii, Blue Mountain from Jamaica. French-roasted, water-processed decaf, organic, shade-grown, fair-trade coffee. Double decaf lattes with no foam, espressos, cappuccinos with half low-fat milk, half cream, sprinkled with chocolate and just a pinch of cinnamon and nutmeg.

I reached my favorite coffeehouse just five minutes from my house. I often went there to sit, drink tea at an outside table, relax, write, and forget about the pockmarked walls of the bedroom in the house of an old lady.

Purple bougainvillea cascades down the whitewashed walls of the corner church. Pierced, tattooed students and conventional businesspeople return from school or work. Mothers push babies in prams.

Just twelve miles away, an old woman rolls out of bed at night to dodge the bullets. My heart aches for her, fighting to recover from her stroke, fighting to retain her dignity. She kicked her grandchildren out of the house, she locked her door, but what can an old frail woman do?

Pray.

CHAPTER 19

I learned that the black community migrated to Richmond from the rural South during the Second World War to work in the booming shipbuilding industry. Richmond had been a mostly rural town of 28,000 but was transformed into an industrial hub when Henry Kaiser opened three shipyards on the waterfront there. The population jumped to 108,000. The men worked in the shipyards and on the railroad. They brought out their families. North Richmond was the only place where blacks were allowed to buy property. The inhabitants grew corn and greens, raised chickens and rabbits, and shared food with one another because they did not have many resources. North Richmond became a settlement of country people. Richmond was a vibrant community filled with the sounds of jazz and blues. Busy nightclubs, theaters, and restaurants like the Dew Drop Inn and Toppers Inn lined the streets. People like John Lee Hooker, Muddy Waters, and T-Bone Walker entertained the shipyard workers. The clubs came to be known as a stop on the Chitlin' Circuit. At this time, of course, segregation was strictly enforced.

After the war, as white soldiers returned, the black workers lost their jobs. New jobs were hard to find, and blacks were not allowed to buy or own homes. Gradually the city and the surrounding areas declined. Chesley Avenue divided North Richmond and the incorporated area south of Chesley. There was no police protection in North Richmond. The Neighborhood House on Chesley Avenue, founded by the American Friends Service Committee, provided a well baby clinic and other health and social services.

The real erosion began with the arrival of drugs, especially crack cocaine in the 1980s. This epidemic brought dreadful violence, shootings, gang and turf warfare, and drug-exposed infants. The strong matriarchal society fell apart as young addicts gave birth to addicted babies. Grandmothers who had worked all their lives and looked forward to a well-earned rest took in these grandchildren in order to keep families together. I have met many such women, some in their eighties, who have raised several generations of children. They are the strongest women I know. Many of them left abusive husbands and threw addicted children out. They raise their grandchildren with love and a strong hand, trying to build a future for them. Life has not beaten them down.

Listening to their stories, I cannot help but think how extremely lucky I am. These women, by virtue of being poor and black, are at the bottom of America's unacknowledged totem pole. I know there have been many times in my life when I have been dismissed because I am a woman. I have experienced this, for instance, when dealing with mechanics who treat me like some kind of idiot when I describe what is wrong with my car. When I see a male doctor I totally forget any symptoms I have and just nod, acquiescing to whatever he says. Only later do I think of questions, or remember what I really wanted to ask.

As is often the case, at the time in my work when I was learning these things about the black community I was presented with opportunities to get to know even more. A doctor requested that I check whether a woman who claimed to need a wheelchair really did.

Sophie lived in Section 8 (subsidized) housing, together with one of her daughters and many grandchildren, ranging in age from toddlers to teenagers. A deep and husky woman's voice answered my knock, calling me to come inside. Upon entering the living room I saw an enormous woman sitting on a black leather couch. Her extremely generous thighs splayed out, leaving little room for anyone else on the couch. To her right was a glass-topped coffee table on which lay a remote control and an ashtray filled to overflowing with cigarette butts. The smell of cigarette smoke permeated every piece of furniture, the carpets, and the curtains.

"Hi," she called. "Come on in. I'd get up, but it's too difficult." She motioned me to sit on a chair opposite the sofa.

She was, for obvious reasons, having great difficulty ambulating. Not only did she suffer from degenerative joint disease, but she was so obese that just standing up required a major effort, let alone taking steps after that. She spent her days smoking and watching TV. The view outside her window was of railway tracks with a litter-strewn patch of grass in front of them. On rainy days the water collected in dark puddles at the sides of the street, and empty cigarette boxes and candy wrappers floated on the surface, like urban boats. When she had to get up she yelled for someone in the house to come so she could hold on to them. Despite this rather strange setup, there was a warmth to her voice and a kind smile on her face that made me immediately feel at ease. My eyes watered from the cigarette smoke, but I just dabbed at them with my tissues as we spoke. One of the questions I had to ask was how she went to the toilet. Because of her size and her joint problems, she might be having difficulty accessing and sitting on the toilet, and I could order her a bedside commode.

"I goes and I sits," she said, and the two of us laughed at the obvious.

She was grateful that eventually a doctor had even considered her plea for a wheelchair. It had taken all her nerve to find a sympathetic doctor: several had insisted there was nothing wrong with her when she told them she had constant pain in her back, hips, and knees.

On one visit, when yet another doctor saying "You seem fine" dismissed her without even a basic physical, she had reached the end of her tether and let fly.

"Don't fuckin' tell me I'm fine, I ain't. My bones ache, I can barely move. I know how the fuck I feel, you don't."

Taken aback, he had sent her for a workup. As well as degenerative joint disease, they found two herniated disks.

We discussed doctors and health care, then moved on to the topic of the current recession, the general sorry "state of the union," unemployment, hopelessness, drugs.

Sophie told me she had three daughters, whom she had raised alone.

She lit up a cigarette, took a drag, and blew the smoke away from my face. "One day my youngest daughter called me. 'Mom,' she said, 'have you heard from Aisha?' She be my oldest daughter. I told her I hadn't heard from her in about a week and she hadn't returned my calls.

"'Come with me to San Francisco, you need to see what's going on.'

"We took the bus to San Francisco and arrived at Aisha's apartment. My granddaughter of three opened the door. I couldn't believe my eyes. That little girl was so hungry, she was near to starvin', cryin' and filthy.

"Lord, I thought, what's goin' on? She didn't know where her mom was. I found some food and made her something to eat, then I bathed her, cleaned her sheets, and put her to sleep. I sat next to her and waited."

Sophie paused to take a deep breath, and then to puff on her cigarette.

"Aisha came home at about two a.m., her eyes rollin' 'round like balls. She saw me and started cryin' and yellin' like a mad person.

"'Don't be mad, Ma, things be so hard. You dunno what it's like to raise a kid alone. You dunno nothin'.'

"Sick at heart, I sat waiting for her to finish. Then, quiet-like, I said, 'Don't you fuckin' tell me what's hard, girl. I raised the three of you alone. I didn't eat so I could feed you. When it was cold I stuffed the holes in my shoes with newspaper, jus' so I could buy y'all shoes and clothes. I know what's hard, and I know I loved y'all and never left you alone. Don't you come to me with your tears, you got a daughter to raise.'"

She stubbed out her cigarette and continued, "I called a poh-liceman friend and told him to come get my granddaughter. What Aisha didn't know was that he took her to my youngest daughter. She thought he took her to a foster home. Then me and my other two girls, we told Aisha we didn't want her around no more, not unless she got straight and cleaned up her act.

"You know what?" She puffed on her cigarette. "That did it. She clean now for seven years. I just dunno what the fuck is wrong these days. Seems like the world has gone crazy."

Sophie did get a wheelchair, making it easier for her to go on doctors' visits and to church on Sundays. She also stopped smoking. Unfortunately, her weight situation did not improve, and in fact she gained even more weight after she quit smoking. Years later I met one of her grandsons and he told me, "She just gave up, life was too hard for her."

CHAPTER 20

Because of my work, I see and experience certain kinds of reality, and then I return home, just ten minutes away, and experience a different one. It was the same in the suburbs of Johannesburg: the streets were quiet except for the occasional hum of the latest model American, British, and Australian cars. Homes were landscaped with lush, beautiful gardens in which turquoise swimming pools and lavender blue jacaranda trees glowed like jewels. Public schools were good. Just a few miles away, Alexander township seethed, a teeming mass of shanty homes, corrugated roofs held down with stones, unbearable poverty, concrete, dirt, red earth, and violence.

My reality, eight miles from Richmond, is quiet and calm. Of course I hear police and fire sirens, but they do not present a constant cacophony. I certainly don't see the clouds of white smoke and flames billowing from the refineries, even though they are not far away. I do not hear the sirens at eleven a.m. on the first Wednesday of the month as the countywide alarm system is tested. I have my garden, and trees line the street. If I am hungry or I just want to go out and socialize, there is every kind of good food available, from anywhere in the world: Italy, India, China, Ethiopia, Eritrea, France, Korea, Japan, the Caribbean, Mexico, West Africa, and on and on.

I live near Berkeley, where many of its citizens are oh so politically correct and self-righteous. The only people who ever attacked me for having the gall to come from South Africa were the white liberals of Berkeley. They attacked me with equal vehemence because not only am I a South African, I am also an Israeli. In Berkeley, the perceived underdog is to be helped or pitied just so long, I notice, as the underdog stays far from their homes. Good Berkeley citizens visit third world countries and report back on child labor, starvation, human rights abuses, the plights of the rain forests, elephants, rhinos, pandas, tigers. But these same people will not go into East or West Oakland, Richmond, San Pablo, or, for that matter, West Berkeley. They do not want to see or hear about their neighbors. It is easier to report on the suffering and abuse of children in the third world than children close by. The world applauds the work these people do on behalf of faraway places. And so, when I sit with them at dinner and relate some of the things I have seen, they cluck their tongues for a moment and then collect money for the children of the endangered Amazon basin.

Most of us hear the statistics on the radio or TV, we read the papers. We are theoretically aware of "downsizing," the sky-rocketing costs of health care, and welfare cuts. Despite this, for many people who still have the security of health insurance and jobs, these statistics are just that—numbers. Surely the lazy people who sponge off the system do not deserve benefits; after all, they have been living off us hard workers for generations. Those people are different from us, distant, apart. Little do people think that soon these statistics will affect almost everyone.

How easy it is to condemn and blame those we don't know, those we hardly ever see, and those with whom we have never spoken.

I attended a Friday night dinner in Albany. As is often the case in the Bay Area, the guests discussed food, or rather, the virtues of eating healthy, organic food. One of the men present asked smugly, speaking about the poor, "Why don't they eat well?"

"Who are the 'they' you are referring to?" I asked, my guts churning as I listened to him pontificate. "Have you ever been to the inner city?"

"No, of course not."

"Why not? It is only five miles from your house. Come with me. We will have to drive, as there is not much public transportation. The few mom-and-pop stores you will see sell fast food, candy, and liquor. Where are they supposed to go for good food?

You won't see banks or supermarkets. The closest ones are at the very least a bus ride or two away. Go inside and look around. The produce is not as good as in the supermarkets in other areas. The vegetables are near to rotting, the quality and cuts of the meat are poorer, and the prices are higher. Many of those people grow their own vegetables, but unfortunately the soil is toxic. They live downwind of the refineries and waste dumps. They fish in the bay nearby, but the fish are full of poisons, and no one has bothered to put signs up in their languages."

I was not invited for dinner again.

CHAPTER 21

Usually, when someone new came to work at the home health agency, they spent a day accompanying one member of the team on visits. One morning the nursing supervisor introduced me to Mimi, the new quality-control person, a former nurse, and asked me to take her with me that day. Mimi was a large, light-skinned black woman with freckles sprinkled across her nose and dyed blonde hair. She was warm, caring, solid, and funny, and I felt safer than usual with her in my car. At those rare times when I drove with either a man or woman of color, I noticed that I felt less conspicuous. I stick out like a sore thumb in most neighborhoods. People on the street have asked if I am a representative of HUD, and children in foster care ask whether I have come to take them back to their mommies.

My first visit that day was to a young man with a malignant brain tumor. He had undergone chemo and radiation therapies, but according to my referral notes, these had not been successful in inhibiting the growth of the tumor. His prognosis was not hopeful. A short while after we left the office, I drove into one of the grittier neighborhoods. Mimi looked at the rundown homes, the pitted roads, and the young guys loitering on the corners.

"Uh-oh, we going here?" asked Mimi.

I parked in front of a bungalow house with a large, broken-down Buick in the garden.

"Oh no," muttered Mimi as we walked to the house.

Strange, I thought to myself, I have been here quite a few times and never felt the sense of anticipation and dread she seems to feel.

"Oh no," she said again as I greeted four muscle-bound teen-aged men walking down the stairs of the home. I knew the guys had been there to help move their friend from his bed to a wheelchair. They would be back later to help him back to bed again.

A beer-bellied white man with a stringy salt-and-pepper beard reaching down to his chest, a greasy shirt, and denim jeans which fell halfway down his liberal-sized butt opened the door. He recognized me, smiled, and beckoned us in, holding out a large hand with nicotine-stained fingers to Mimi.

"Come on in, everyone's inside." He meant everyone. At least six adolescent girls, all in various stages of pregnancy, lounged around on the sofa and chairs. I could never keep count of the young children running around. At least four of them remembered me and jumped into my arms and clung to my legs.

I heard Mimi's "oh no" behind me.

While we waited for Old Mother Hubbard (as I had privately named the mother of the young man) to come out of the bathroom, Mimi addressed a general question in the vicinity of the young girls.

"Why y'all not in school?"

They looked at her, shrugged their shoulders, and turned back to watch *The Jerry Springer Show.* Today's theme: "mothers who slept with their daughters' boyfriends." Porcupine quills of anger shot out from Mimi.

It was scenes such as this one that made me realize how poor public education is, certainly in West County. These girls did not seem interested in the world around them, or in books. Obviously school was not good enough to keep them attending. And they were all pregnant. They never had sex education. "Just say no" does not work with sex or drugs.

Old Mother Hubbard came in smiling. She'd worked her night shift, then come home to care for two of her sons, one with cancer and the other in another room with a broken leg and hip. Every day she cooked, cleaned, shopped, bathed, dressed the children, and cared for her sons, smiling and joking all the while. At night she worked as a nursing aide. The dying son's young and very pregnant girlfriend and their two-year-old son stayed in his bedroom.

He was joking with his girlfriend and one of his sisters, a school bus driver, when we walked in. His girlfriend obviously was in a state of denial about his dire prognosis, despite the fact that the tumor was causing his forehead to bulge and distort his face, making his eyes appear like slits. Excitedly she told me they were planning to move back to Oakland as soon as he got better. Their two-year-old bounced on the bed. Other kids ran in and out. All the young teens were totally engrossed in watching the strange species of people on *Jerry Springer* scream obscenities and pull each other's hair. From time to time those in the room laughed and made comments. "She fixin' to fight! Go, bitch! Yeah, get down! Get dirty."

The patient himself told Mimi and me he was feeling fine and fixing to leave and go back to Oakland. He didn't need no services now that he was getting better.

Well, good, I thought, that is the power of positive thinking.

After we left this bedlam, Mimi declared she needed food. Over a hamburger at Red Onion she told me she had no patience for all that crap. "Did you see his diamond ring and earring? He must have been a dealer. At least now there will be one less on the streets. And those young girls? That grandma should whup each and every one of them and get their sorry asses back to school."

I'd have thought she would be more compassionate. To me he was a human being, a son, a father who was desperately ill.

"Let me tell you a story," she said, sipping a Coke and dipping a fry into ketchup. "My middle daughter had four kids. One day my niece of six was visiting, and she told me and my husband that the other night her baby sister of six months woke up howlin', cryin'. My niece went to wake her momma, but she and her man were out cold and neither of them woke up, even though she shouted and banged her little hands on them. My little bitty niece said she gave her baby sister milk and changed her diaper." Mimi chomped on a fry. "And that's how I found out my daughter was a crackhead.

"I called a doctor friend and told him I was bringing my daughter in to have her tubes tied. I dragged her out of her house, shoved her into my car, and drove with her kicking and screaming all the way to the hospital.

"'You can't do this,' she cried. 'I got my rights.'

"'Shut up,' I told her. 'You lost your rights the moment you brought four children into the world. I don't want to hear about rights. You can go ahead and kill yourself, because you are dead to me and your father anyway.'

"Her tubes were tied, so at least she can't have more kids— because she still uses dope. We adopted her children."

She opened her handbag and pulled out a well-worn photo album. Proudly she showed me pictures of their comfortable suburban home with a large yard and swimming pool. Photos of the kids swimming, playing, in school, dressed for church, attending parties. Sometimes she brought the kids into the office. Every Sunday she and her husband took them to Bible school. With obvious delight she told everyone in our office of their progress in school.

Tragically, two years after she told me this story Mimi discovered she had breast cancer. Seven months later it had progressed to her lungs and spinal column. Eight months after she was diagnosed, she passed away. The children remain with Mimi's husband. Their mother still alternates between being clean and using drugs.

Mimi's was the first funeral I attended here in America. When I arrived at the mortuary in Oakland I was ushered in by solemn men in black suits and dark red ties. I saw something in white in the front. It was far away and I didn't have my glasses on. The place was crowded and silent. I sat down and put on my glasses and looked again, and very nearly screamed—loud, and at great length. It was Mimi, lying on her back in an open coffin lined with white, padded satin. I had never seen anything like it. I hastily averted my eyes and sat quietly, my heart beating fast.

My very white flesh broke out in goose bumps. I didn't see anyone I knew well enough to ask what on earth was going on. At
the end of an emotional, song-filled, moving ceremony, during
which Mimi necessarily remained in repose, the solemn-looking
men came and gestured to the people sitting alongside me. They
stood up and I followed as they shuffled along to what I thought
would be the exit. Soon I realized I was following them as they
filed past that thing. I glanced inside at Mimi, who resembled a
figure at Madame Tussaud's, hair fluffed, rouge on her cheeks
and lips, lying on her back in a white dress, cushioned in gleam-
ing white satin.

Before that day, the only funerals I had been to were in Israel.
There the bodies were wrapped in shrouds and placed directly
in the dug-up earth, and then mourners shoveled dirt over the
bodies. The soldiers were laid to rest in simple pine coffins: we
did not see their violated corpses.

"For dust you are and to dust you shall return."

CHAPTER 22

His gray-green eyes, rimmed by dark lashes, bored right through me, tunneling inside, searching for something he could tear away from me. That stare caused my blood to drain from my legs to my feet, rooting me to my spot in front of the hospital bed. The anger, hatred, and hostility in his eyes I could deal with. It was something else I could not define that made the hairs on the back of my neck prickle.

Not fifteen minutes before, on that pleasant fall afternoon, I had driven through wide, tree-lined streets with the names Diamond, Emerald, Turquoise, Amber, Beryl, Jasper, Lapis, Onyx, and Pearl. Strings of jewels and semiprecious stones. The leaves had begun to change color, wine red, brown, yellow, and they rustled softly as a gentle breeze moved through them.

I followed the directions I had been given by the referring nurse. The road curved upwards, looping gently to the left. I saw the number of the stucco, two-story home and parked alongside the curb. As I entered the mileage into my logbook I glanced into my rear-view mirror and was surprised to see a police car pull up behind me. I panicked for a moment, wondering what I had done, but then I realized the lights were not flashing and I had not heard a siren. I thought that it must be a police officer come home for a cup of coffee, until I saw two armed policemen enter the very house I was to visit. Now what to do? Should I go in or drive away and come back another time? Just an hour before, I had arranged with the patient's aunt to come at this time, so it should be okay to go in, I reasoned.

I had been sent to this home in Hercules to evaluate a twenty-year-old man who was paralyzed as a result of gunshots. Against medical advice he'd had a friend spirit him away from the rehabilitation hospital. His mother refused to let him stay with her. His grandmother, who lived in a different home, also would not take him in. An aunt who lived in Hercules with her husband and teenage daughter agreed to let him stay. These two refusals from his closest family made me wonder what kind of person I would be dealing with. Also, Big Bill had seen him once and been told to leave. Bill thought maybe I could make some headway with him.

The front door was ajar, and I looked inside the house at what appeared to be a kitchen, which led to a den or living room. The cops were inside the living room, but their firearms remained in their holsters, so I walked up the pathway and stood at the open door.

"Come in," said an attractive older woman standing next to a young man lying in a hospital bed in the living room. "I spoke to you on the phone."

I walked through the pleasant kitchen, noticing the lovely African violet plants on the white windowsills. The living room was sunny and bright. Glass sliding doors opened to an outside patio on which a white table and lawn chairs covered with yellow cushions stood under a yellow and white striped umbrella, affording lovely views of the colorful garden and surrounding hills. The hospital bed had obviously been placed in this room since the arrival of the patient.

His aunt and I shook hands as if nothing untoward were happening. She introduced me to her daughter and to the young man, Victor, who lay in the hospital bed.

"Me and my daughter are off to court. I hope to catch you later today, or next time." Walking out of the house together with the policemen, she and her daughter smiled pleasantly, leaving me alone with the young man.

I addressed the space in front of Victor and told him why I had come.

He opened his eyes and stared at me and through me. The side of his left lip curled upwards. A smile maybe?

His gray-green eyes flashed.

"If you can't get me an electric wheelchair, you can get out."
These were his first words.

Swallowing hard, I told him I could assist, but first I had to ask questions and complete an evaluation so that I could order the appropriate equipment.

Gray-green darts of anger flew toward me.

"Why should I talk to you? All I want is a chair. Anyway, you should know what I can or can't do, isn't it written down in your papers?"

I didn't tell him, but there was conflicting information in the referral papers. It stated that he is a quadriplegic, and further down the page, a paraplegic. I truly did need to assess whether or not he had any movement left in his shoulders and arms (UEs—the acronym for upper extremities).

He spoke in a loud, threatening tone that I chose to ignore. I noticed that he had somehow managed to maneuver the sheet further up his face, covering his mouth. It was obvious he had some movement left. He certainly didn't appear to be a high-level quadriplegic—that is, one with spinal cord injuries in the cervical vertebrae—because he would not have the amount of movement I had noticed. I knew that with correct exercise and proper splinting on his hands, he would be able to perform any number of activities. In fact, I thought, maybe as an incentive I should tell him that he might even be able to shoot again. I decided, however, against giving him this piece of good news.

"I'm not gonna talk to you, or show you anything. Get the hell out. Go away."

This time he shouted and turned his head away from me, toward the bedrails on his right side. The flintlike tone in his voice and the gray-green barbs that hovered between us unnerved me yet again. I was pleased he was in no position to hurt me. I would tell Big Bill this was not a person with whom one could "make headway."

I began to understand why his family had not taken him back and wondered how long his aunt would keep him.

"Get the hell out."

He made himself clear. I needed to respect that.

"Okay," I said. "My card is on the kitchen counter. Your aunt can call if you change your mind."

I walked to my car. I knew he was angry—who wouldn't be? In less than a nanosecond, his life had changed forever. He had become a prisoner in his own body, a dreadful thing to happen to anyone. But, I thought, he had probably not been shot for helping a little old lady across the street. Someone did not want him around. He obviously had not thought of the consequences to his actions. This was the result, now it was up to him to choose how to proceed.

Suddenly I understood what it was that had caused the hairs on my neck to prickle, and what had so unnerved me when I first stood before him. It was the presence of evil.

I have seen people in the most abysmal of conditions: victims of violence and accidents; people, old and young, with dreadful, debilitating diseases. I see angry, confused, hostile, sad people, but I had never come across anyone quite like this young man. I had stared into the face of evil: an entity, a force, that sucks up any humanity or compassion that presents itself. Evil is threatened by these counterforces. It sucks them in so that it can survive and gain strength. It will destroy everything in its path, including the entity it inhabits. Evil had invaded this young man, and it would seep out and hurt his family, and those trying to assist.

His salvation did not lie in people outside of himself. If he did not find the kernel of resilience and good inside of himself, he would shrivel and die.

Saddened and shaken to the pit of my stomach, I drove away, wondering yet again how I, a Jewish girl from South Africa and Israel, had arrived at this juncture, pondering upon the nature of good and evil in the rolling hills of Hercules, in northern California.

The only answer I had to these weighty questions was that I had absolutely no idea. Life presents many questions, and answers are not always found. Furthermore, I needed to concentrate on my driving and get to the next patient, but the evil green eyes floated in my mind's eye. Each time I saw them there, my flesh felt like it was withdrawing, leaving me raw, exposed, and vulnerable.

CHAPTER 23

Victor was paralyzed in a shooting. Probably revenge shootings had already occurred. Most likely some other young man or men had been wounded or killed, or would be, soon. Impromptu altars would be set up in front of a fence, outside a house, an alley, a driveway. A photo of the dead person, with his or her name and "R.I.P." written in crude block letters. Fading bouquets, candles, handwritten notes, bottles of alcohol, balloons, and stuffed animals.

The full impact of violence, sometimes gang-related, sometimes not, jumps from the headlines of the daily papers—or, sadly, more often from the back pages, scrunched between articles on the economy, terrorism, and wars. These daily articles become real after I meet the perpetrators and the victims. Usually a perpetrator is a victim as well.

Frequently, when a particularly heinous crime is committed, the neighbors of the perpetrator say something like "But he was so nice. Who would have thought? He mowed his lawn, smiled at our children. He was so quiet," and so on. Now I feel the same way those surprised neighbors do. I meet people whose names appear in papers, and I find out that they are for the most part, despite their bravado, regular young men or women. I get to know them and meet their children, mothers, sometimes fathers, and friends, whom they sometimes refer to as colleagues.

I do not recall any gunshot victims telling me why they had been shot, though I remember others offering opinions. If the victims remember the shooting, they simply recount the incident: "I heard a pow-pow and saw my colleague fall down next to me. Man, I didn't never think I would see that."

Sometimes during the course of a conversation I hear a phrase or something that leaves me saddened, stunned, and infuriated.

"He was shot 'cause he owed the dealer twenty dollars."

"He dissed my girlfriend."

"I shouldn't have been on that corner."

"That was the second time I was shot this year. The first time the bullet just grazed me."

"A car came up and a man leaned out and pumped lead into me."

Life has no value. These are young people with little or no education, without hope or aspirations. A large number are from single parent homes, and their mothers are often very young. Many were raised in numerous foster homes. Bullets don't discriminate, and the victims make up a "rainbow nation" of white, black, Latino, Asian, male, female, middle-aged, but most often heartbreakingly young. Probably the only time anyone ever really looked at them was in those nanoseconds before they pulled the trigger or stood on the other side of the gun. Some of the youth now killing each other were born addicted to drugs, the unplanned offspring of addicts, and because of pre-natal brain damage and environmental trauma they are unable to distinguish between right and wrong, or cause and effect.

It is heartrending to watch people who have suddenly become paralyzed or otherwise incapacitated as they slowly, painstakingly, and often with reluctance and anger relearn to get out of bed, bathe, and dress.

One rainy morning I watched a young man who, until just a couple of months before, had been completely healthy and, according to his mom, a lieutenant in a gang. A shooting had left him paralyzed from the waist down. He was in a rehabilitation hospital after the injury and had now returned home. In the rehab hospital he had worked with a "stupid" male therapist. Apparently a "dumb bitch" had also instructed him. He was not used to taking orders from anyone, let alone a woman. And now there I stood, helping him plan his movements and negotiate transfers. I am sure he had also suffered brain damage, because motor planning was not one of his strengths. It took him the better part of an hour to sit up in his twin-size bed by raising his once muscular arms to reach for the overhead trapeze bar. Then he hitched himself to a sitting position and used his arms to shift his body until he reached the edge of the bed. From there he could grab the bar on the far side of the wheelchair positioned next to the bed and swing into the chair. He was sweating uncontrollably, which was because of the damage to his autonomic nervous system, and he had not yet begun to dress himself. He struggled, sweated, cursed, tried to pull on his pants, and gave up, cursing at his long-suffering mother, who then put on his clothes.

Big Bill to the rescue, I thought, I wished he could be cloned. He could go the next time, maybe he wouldn't be cursed at. Too bad most people in the helping professions are women. Men are sorely needed.

CHAPTER 24

I worked with a little girl whom I grew to love dearly. During the course of the time we spent together, I learned to know her parents, and her grandmothers. One beautiful, blossom-filled Sunday in spring I received a phone call from the family to tell me that her twenty-six-year-old daddy, Deshawn, had been killed the night before, shot to death on the streets of his hometown.

The funeral parlor was packed. The overflow crowd stood in the street and in clusters on the corners—three hundred people, at least. Young women, hair in braids and coils, held tiny babies whose braided hair was decorated with colorful barrettes, headbands, and beads. Zigzag parts, spiral parts, works of art. Old women in hats limped in, using canes. The women and girls dressed in somber black, white, green, low-cut tops, lots of bling, high heels, skin in all shades of dark, some with tattoos of numbers or names engraved into their flesh. Young men in dreads, close-shaved heads, grillz (gold teeth), gold chains, baggy pants, enormous sports jackets in red, white, and blue, smart suits. They hit each other on their backs, exchanged elaborate handshakes, and wiped away tears. Many wore shirts with a picture of Deshawn silkscreened on the front.

From where I stood in the foyer of the funeral home, I could hardly hear the choir as it began singing, so I wormed my way into the crowded parlor. The pews were packed, the sidewalls lined deep with mourners. The choir sang, a cappella, as people stood and clapped and punched the air with raised arms and clenched fists, crying "Hallelujah" and "Jesus."

I caught sight of Deshawn lying in a white-satin-lined casket but quickly looked the other way, still not used to seeing bodies lying so still and waxy-looking. A woman pastor rose, pacing back and forth, stabbing at the air with her hands, stamping her feet, shouting something about heaven and hell and being ready to meet our Lord. Life isn't meant to be easy, she said, but the Lord is with us when we get up and when we fall down. Mourners sobbed, and shouted, and suddenly all around me the sound of beautiful voices filled the air in a spiritual vaguely familiar to me. "Going down yonder to be with my Lord" and "I will trust in the Lord until I die." The voices swelled and rose and fell, and people clapped and swayed, and I was carried away to scenes of slaves in sheds singing their hurt and their sorrows away. I was transported to South Africa, different music, different songs, but that same wave of music lifting troubled spirits.

And so Deshawn became just one more name in the paper, one more statistic.

When I lived through the Yom Kippur War in Israel in my twenties, the women sat together in our rooms at night, drinking endless cups of coffee while we listened to the news and the daily tally of dead and wounded soldiers. Cynically we joked that any man who made it to thirty years of age would be lucky. My husband and three other members of our kibbutz had already been killed. I never dreamed this would happen again, especially in a faraway country not at war.

My friends in the office who began working there long before me had been to countless funerals. All too often they were for victims of violence, the sons and sometimes the daughters of clerical workers and nurses. I began to recognize that we were working and dealing with a community in constant trauma, something I was all too familiar with. Now, daily, I encounter the shadow side of America, just a few minutes from where I live. Killings, retaliations, more killings, and I think, But America is not at war, young men should go on living to a ripe old age. Every year I visit Israel and find it ironic that people here ask whether I am scared to go there. I explain that almost daily I see far worse things than I ever see in Israel. I realize that America is at war, with itself, and the numbers of victims, bereaved parents, and traumatized children mount daily.

CHAPTER 25

A woman of twenty-two was shot while jumping over a fence during a crack deal gone bad. She was paralyzed from the neck down and had recently returned home after a long stint in a rehabilitation hospital. She and her three children lived with her parents in North Richmond.

On my first visit, in the pouring rain, I saw a rusty, battered truck parked outside the house. As I sloshed through puddles, the man sitting in the truck opened the door and stepped out. He was painfully thin and stooped. A salt-and-pepper beard reached down to his hollow chest. In one hand he held a beer can, in the other a cigarette.

"Hi." His greeting was followed by a lengthy outburst of coughing. "You come to see my daughter?" Cough, cough, cough.

"Yes," I said.

"Okay (cough, cough, cough), go upstairs," he said, pointing to a house close by, "and bang loudly, the bell doesn't work and it's noisy inside."

I climbed the fourteen steps leading to the front door. From inside I heard the sound of children's voices over what sounded like the blaring of MTV. I knocked as hard as I could, skinning my knuckles, until a tall, wiry young woman opened the door.

"You come to see my sister? Come this way," she said.

A little girl with unruly hair bundled up in a scrunchie rode a tricycle in circles around the bare wooden floor. Two young boys sat on the floor, their eyes glued to MTV.

The client's sister led me to a bedroom, the very walls and floor of which vibrated from the sound of hip-hop booming from the radio that stood on a table next to the bed. The pretty young woman lying on top of the bed was either still in shock about the reality of her condition, or in complete denial, or very stupid: according to her everything was fine, and she was sure that one day she would be able to move her limbs again. The kids playing in the living room were hers, she told me, and she wanted to move into a cottage in the backyard with them. Her sister sat on the edge of the bed. A few minutes later her mom came from out of the kitchen to join us.

At one point in our conversation I asked the young woman whether she remembered anything about the shooting.

"I saw a corridor of light," she said. "My brother was at the other end and he told me I have to go back." This brother, she then added, had been shot and killed two years before in a drug-related fight. Another brother was killed while on active duty in the Philippines, but she hadn't seen him in the corridor.

How, I wondered, did her parents cope with all this tragedy? Her mom worked as a teacher's aide in the mornings and then came home to look after her daughter and her grandchildren. She shrugged her shoulders philosophically when I asked her, saying she manages with the help of the Lord. The father drank beer in a truck outside their home and planned the remodeling of the cottage for his daughter and her children. He wanted suggestions for accommodating the wheelchair, such as kitchen shelves she could reach, and a shower and toilet she could wheel herself into.

On a subsequent visit a young man with slicked-back hair sat next to a teenage girl in the bedroom. The patient graciously introduced us. "This is my brother Joe and his girlfriend." They nodded at me. "And this is my therapist."

Fanned out like a deck of cards on a table in front of them were about ten driver's licenses. From the photos I saw they did not belong to anyone in the immediate vicinity. I had recently been the victim of identity theft, and someone had spent fifteen thousand dollars posing as me. I scrutinized the licenses and wondered if I would see myself there, alongside the other faces peering from the top of the table. What surprised me was that no one made any effort to cover them while I was there. Of course, I was not sure that anything illegal was happening, and besides, it was none of my business.

This way of life was as normal to these young people as getting an education and going to work had been to me.

. . .

In the *OT Week* magazine of August 26, 1999, was a short article from the *Journal of the American Medical Association*. It bore the title "Gunshot Injuries Cost Taxpayers." According to this article:

> Scientists, using data from multiple sources, estimated a median cost of $17,000 per gunshot injury. Of the 134,445 injuries reported in 1994, which accounted for $2.3 billion in lifetime medical costs, taxpayer-funded government paid $1.1 billion or 49% of the costs…The difference between fatal and nonfatal hospitalized gunshot injury cases highlights the magnitude of follow-up treatment costs. In non-fatal cases, the majority of health spending occurs after the patient has been discharged from the hospital.

Of course, the damage resulting from the violence that kills and injures such a horrifyingly large number of people is definitely not just measured monetarily. I think of the psychological fallout around our patients and all of those who are affected: their families and friends, the traumatized children who need to talk about the violence they see. What about the police, sheriffs, EMTs, doctors, nurses, therapists? We too are affected; we also need to talk. Just one death, or one individual left with traumatic brain injury or paralyzed for life, affects hundreds. And health-care professionals see many more than just one.

I saw so many gunshot-wound cases, nearly all of them young men and women, that I took up the rather morbid activity of cutting out the small paragraphs about them buried in the daily newspapers. For example:

> Police found EG, 38, and KH, 27, both of Richmond,
> injured in the ——— block of ——— Street around 8:15
> a.m. Anyone with any knowledge, please call ———.

I cut these out because of the key word, "injured" (not dead), because I knew they would eventually be referred to us.

Indeed, one afternoon I found myself sitting next to KH, a young woman who had been shot in the leg a minor injury, luckily. She was referred a week after I had read the short paragraph about her and a man who had been sitting in a car when they were shot. I mentioned that I had read about it in the paper.

"Yeah," she said, proudly, "my aunt called from San Francisco because she saw it also."

Fifteen minutes of fame.

CHAPTER 26

After spending a day hearing heartrending stories, I find it hard to shake off my day's work. When I began working as a therapist, I had just begun a relationship with a really kind and sweet man. I felt supported when he asked about my work. He was concerned about my working in dangerous areas. That caring was new for me, as I had become so accustomed to living alone. It was comforting to have someone concerned about me and my whereabouts. He called during the day, also, especially when he heard reports in the news of shootings and accidents. I phoned him when I got home in the evenings and shared my stories.

At that time I was also involved in an Israeli peace group, "Yesh Gvul" (which means "there is a border, or a limit"). We raised money to support the soldiers who were sent to jail for refusing to fight in the Occupied Territories. The group was conducting a fundraising tour and requested that I, with a former soldier who had been jailed, tour the country, explaining our cause. My friend helped with the logistics of our hectic tour of the southern and northwestern states and took care of my home while I was on the road. Soon after I returned, my work intensified. My caseload increased and there seemed to be more and more difficult cases, along with pending budget cuts. I came home depleted, and suddenly, without warning, the man changed. He stopped checking in during the day and spent all his time lying in bed, claiming he did not feel well. This was a new side to him that appeared out of the blue. His shadow loomed large, craggy, and fierce, and I found it increasingly difficult to deal with his outbursts and unpredictability. It was bad enough managing my challenging job; I did not have the energy to deal with his moods when I came home. Besides, what had happened, why was he not well all the time? I found it hard to muster up compassion for him when I saw so many people who were battling chronic or terminal diseases. But nevertheless, for some strange reason, I remained in this relationship, even though I was expert at solving other people's problems.

I was so good at giving advice to others. When the clerk appeared with welts and bruises on her arms and body, it was obvious that she should leave her latest abuser, but she didn't, not for a long time.

"He is stressed," she said. "He didn't mean it." He sent flowers to the office and bought her a puppy, then broke her arm. Still she didn't leave. It was only when he hit her son that she had a restraining order put on him.

In no way did I see any connection between her relationship and mine. She was being abused physically. Of course she should leave him.

I saw a woman in Rodeo whose boyfriend deliberately drove his truck over her. She suffered a shattered pelvis, broken arms, hands, and right femur. When I went to see her she had recently come out of the hospital and was living with her brother. We sat and talked in a room painted deep purple. Soon I realized she was extremely depressed. She cried and cried. I found this totally understandable. I too would be crying under such circumstances. Moreover, she told me that social services had removed her two kids, who were now living with her sister in another town. She sobbed, and I began to distinguish some words between her sobs. "Jimmie," I heard repeatedly, "I want my Jimmie back." I thought Jimmie was her son.

"I can't live without my Jimmie." After we had talked some more, it dawned on me that Jimmie was her erstwhile boyfriend.

I was shocked and angry. "You want him back? He tried to kill you!"

"Yes," she sobbed, "but after he ran me over, he called the ambulance."

Again I could not see any connection between us. No one was trying to run me over. I was being abused verbally, not physically, and I also had excuses: it will be better when he is working again; he is depressed because he is having a hard time finding work—that is why he doesn't get up.

So often, my patients' lives reflected what was taking place in my life, but their lives seemed so very extreme that, although a mirror was held up for me, I could not see my reflection.

. . .

While my relationship deteriorated, I was sent to see a man who had undergone hip replacement surgery. He and his wife lived in a small home in San Pablo. One day I arrived to find their home in total disarray. A side window was shattered and shards of glass, spread out on the driveway, glittered in the washed-out sunlight. Papers, books, and items of clothing were strewn over the shag carpet in the living room. His wife sat on their old lumpy sofa, chain-smoking. I sat next to her while they told me about their son: they had a restraining order against him, but last night he had turned up drunk and abusive, messed up their home, and stolen her Susan B. Anthony dollars, the only item of value she had. They had called the police and then put him on a train out of the area, with no return ticket.

I left them, thinking about what had happened. They loved their son, but he was an alcoholic, and nothing they had tried could help him. Sending him away was difficult for them, but it was the only thing they could do to prevent him from hurting them or their property anymore. Nothing had been stolen from me, except for my energy. The part of me that sustained me and kept me going was being eroded, but still I stumbled along in this strange relationship, unable to break it off. I thought that when he found a job and had a routine, things would improve. Eventually he found a well-paying job. He began working, but his behavior did not improve.

CHAPTER 27

The patient, Brenda, in her early forties, was mildly obese. We sat in the living room of the second-floor apartment she shared with her four teenage children. She sat on a dilapidated easy chair, the only one in the room. I sat on a plastic lawn chair, clipboard in hand. Seated in front of her on a stool was a wiry, slender woman, Jacky.

The apartment was modest. Besides the chairs in the living room, there was a formica table, an ancient black-and-white television set, and photos of Brenda's children, which decorated one wall. This was the week before Christmas, and she had placed a small plastic tree on the table, draped strands of tinsel around it, and sprinkled glitter on the branches.

Brenda supplemented her welfare money by braiding people's hair. This requires a certain amount of dexterity and upper extremity endurance, and because of her illness, myasthenia gravis, which is an autoimmune neuromuscular disorder characterized by fatigue of muscles, most days it was a major task for her to raise her arms at all. But today she felt slightly better, so she was able to braid Jacky's hair during my visit.

Brenda had a deep voice, and she spoke in a rhythmic cadence. "I was born in the Virgin Islands. I married at twenty, on the island of St. Thomas. In the beginning, all was well. We had four children. We worked hard and were content and happy. After about five years we moved to America, because my husband had family here. He found a job in Richmond. I worked as an assistant in a nursery school.

"It happened so slow," she said. I noticed her breathing was becoming faster and more shallow, which confirmed my suspicion that some of her respiratory symptoms were stress-induced.

"It was like I thought maybe I was crazy. His behavior changed. If I hadn't gotten dinner ready by the time he came home, or if he didn't like it, he started to shout and to hit me. He never did that before, so I thought I was a bad wife. I kept the house spotless, I cooked, I did everything I could to be perfect, but you know, he just hit me more and more."

"Uh-uh," responded Jacky, "we think we be bad. We're not, you know."

Brenda continued, "He began to curse and yell at me in front of the kids. Sometimes I called the police, but then when they came, I didn't have it in me to see him go to jail, so I dropped the charges."

"Oh no," said Jacky. I felt my own heart beating faster, listening to this dreadful tale.

"But still, things got worse. One time he knocked me down on the bathroom floor, filled a large pot with hot water, and poured it over me. Three times he filled it, three times he poured. I hurt so much, inside and outside, but I kept quiet.

"I knew I was bad, otherwise this wouldn't be happening. I prayed for patience, and to become a better person. You know, I didn't know he was using crack. It made him crazier and crazier. He was laid off work. He demanded the money I earned and used it to buy drugs. When I realized what he was doing, I hid the money so I could use it for food and rent."

Jacky nodded sympathetically all the while. "I know. It's bad."

"When I was away at work he'd find the money. He used to pay the bills, but one day I came home and found our lights and gas were cut off, and the phone service was stopped. I found extra work cleaning houses to try and pay rent. Then we were evicted. Sixteen years of this, and all the time I thought I was a bad wife and mother. But one day, after another eviction notice, and another round of him hitting me, I grabbed my kids and ran to a battered women's shelter. That place saved our lives. I went into counseling. Slowly I came to understand that I was not the cause of his behavior, and I had no reason to put up with it. It took time, but we're divorced now, and he's not allowed here."

Her breathing became slightly easier once she stopped talking. I showed her how to take deep, calming breaths. In fact, I was breathing deeply myself. Jacky's hands were folded in her lap. "Uh-uh, honey," she said, "it wasn't you. It never is. You should have laid charges when the poh-lice came."

"I was ashamed, and I felt I couldn't send him to jail."

"My husband hit me, too," said Jacky. "I called the poh-lice and I let them take him to jail. He didn't think I would do that, but I wanted him to go, that's where he belonged."

My head followed each woman in turn as they spoke. Slowly it turned, back and forth. I didn't hear anger, just a kind of bitterness, and relief that they could share these awful experiences. It was like listening to friends discussing which schools their kids should attend, and the latest movie they had seen. Just another conversation between women.

I asked Jacky whether her husband hit her after he came out of jail.

"Yes, he came back home and hit me, but honey, he won't do that no more—I shot him."

The three of us laughed uproariously. A glow of female understanding and camaraderie filled the bare room. Sunlight filtered through the lace curtains. The glitter on the small Christmas tree sparkled.

. . .

It was Brenda and Jacky who, through their stories, gave me the strength and courage to end my relationship that very same day. I drove home refreshed, delighted to see, just ahead, a car with the bumper sticker "I'm out of estrogen and I have a gun." Right on, that I could relate to. Surprisingly soon after the relationship ended, my energy returned. Luckily, I have always had lots of friends—in popular parlance, "a good support system"—with whom I speak and go hiking, bird watching, and to movies and museums. I attend a gym, do yoga, and many a Friday night meet coworkers to eat, laugh, drink, and forget the week over a margarita.

For many years I lived in a little cottage in North Oakland. My landlady, who lived in the main house, was Italian, and I am convinced she buried family members in her yard, because the soil was so rich and fertile. Whatever I planted grew in lush abundance: zucchini, tomatoes, beans, and herbs. One of my greatest joys was growing granadillas (passion fruit). A friend of mine who has a farm in East Palo Alto ordered the seeds from South Africa and gave me some, knowing how much I loved the fruit. Carefully I tended the seeds, placing them in egg cartons until small shoots appeared, and then I planted them in the magic soil next to a wooden fence. The first year, the vine grew and flowers appeared, but no fruit. The next year, the vine was larger, the flowers came earlier, and then, wonder of wonders, I saw the fruit appear, green at first, then dark purple. Impatiently I waited until the skin wrinkled. Plucking a perfect specimen, I sunk my teeth into the tough skin, and bit down. The sweet and sour yellow juice filled my mouth, and I remembered South African summer vacations, the golden sand so hot it burnt the undersides of my feet, and the embrace of wild surf. I crunched down on the black pips, eyes closed, savoring each drop. That year I counted one hundred granadillas that I shared with South African friends only. The next year I stopped counting, because I had so many. I froze the juice to use later, in fruit salads and homemade ice cream. Whenever a wave of nostalgia overcame me, or when I saw one single granadilla on sale for two and a half dollars, I went back home to gaze at my vine.

My landlady raised vegetables and tended a small patch of corn. In the evenings I came home to a garden and cottage redolent with the comforting aroma of garlic, enveloping our haven like a security blanket. I usually found her in the garden, apparently moving her large body with great effort, judging by the accompanying sighs and groans, watering, weeding, and cutting her crops. One fogless summer evening I came home to find her watering, groaning, and sighing—nothing untoward.

"How are you?" I asked her.

"Not too good, not too good," she said, breathing heavily, but she always said this. That night I heard a commotion, voices, cars, people going in and out of the house, but again, that was not unusual. She had raised five ne'er-do-well sons, who visited her at all hours and occasionally stayed there when they fought with their wives or girlfriends. When I left for work the next morning, the nicest of them was slowly treading up the stairs to her front door. He saw me and told me that she had died just a few hours before. The house was quickly sold and the new owners raised my rent by a ridiculous amount, so I was forced to move. Luckily, I found a place in Albany, just a ten-minute drive from Richmond, where I now worked full time. There, too, I moved into an apartment in which I could garden. This time I planted fragrant and hardy herbs like lavender, thyme, oregano, marjoram, and rosemary, and a rosebush, because it was an endless delight to come home, close my eyes, and allow the aromas to wash away lingering remnants of the day.

CHAPTER 28

Some people have so many diseases it is a miracle they keep going. The body has a truly miraculous capacity for rejuvenation, and the will to survive is very strong. I have seen patients with chronic obstructive pulmonary disease (COPD), emphysema, lung cancer, hypertension, diabetes, kidney failure, liver failure—in other words, lifestyle-related diseases—who continue to smoke, drink, abuse drugs, and eat the wrong foods. Nothing short of death will stop their relentless path to self-destruction.

When I was growing up, the few times my father drank too much became anecdotes in my family's lore, stories about my dad's amusing eccentricities which we retold and laughed at during extended family get-togethers. Except for these rare occasions, and the shocking and sad case of our neighbor, a kind man who told good jokes and stuttered, and who gassed himself in his car one night, apparently as a result of his alcoholism, my exposure to addictions was blissfully limited. Seeing the pain of addiction firsthand in my work has made me somewhat less judgmental and slightly more compassionate; however, the actions of addicts are still hard for me to comprehend.

Nancy was a woman in her mid-fifties suffering from COPD, diabetes, hypertension, alcoholism, and addiction to nicotine. She lived in a tiny, one-room home in San Pablo that she shared with a friend, a pleasant, white-bearded, long-haired man who also smoked incessantly.

The first time I saw Nancy was through the pall of smoke that permeated the house, the smell clinging to the carpets, curtains, and bedclothes like leeches. She lay in bed, smoking. Nancy must have been beautiful once. Her hair was still thick and black, her eyes startlingly blue, her skin the color of cream. But her eyes watered, and red veins mapped the journey of her life on her pale, wrinkled cheeks. The skin on her arms and upper chest hung off her bones like crinkly paper, and her fingers and teeth were stained a permanent dirty mustard color. She gestured for me to sit, but other than on the edge of her unkempt bed I could not find a spot, so I remained standing, leaning against a wall for support. Her bed was flush against the wall. Packets of cigarettes, empty Jack Daniels bottles, and six-packs of soda were strewn on the floor, along with old newspapers, tabloid magazines, and phone and TV cords. On the other side of the tiny room, against the wall, stood overflowing chests of drawers, a vanity covered with ashtrays piled high with butts, medications, inhalers, and random articles of clothing—a bra, a crumpled blouse, a gown.

Nancy, between coughing and gasping for breath, stated she did not need anything. She used her thin, shaky hands to steady herself on any available object when she walked the ten steps to her bathroom. She was obviously a private person and was not interested in interference. She wanted to drink and smoke in peace.

A few months later a nurse asked me to go back because Nancy was dying, and she said her caregiver needed instructions in sponge bathing her and assisting with bed mobility to prevent pressure sores.

Nancy lay on her back in a hospital bed. Her even skinnier arms, covered loosely with yellow parchment, were folded tightly over her chest. She was hooked up to oxygen twenty-four hours a day, making smoking not only impossible but dangerous as well. She wafted in and out of consciousness.

I asked Nancy whether she was drinking. I meant fluids like water, tea, or juice. Nancy understood differently.

"Not anymore," she replied.

CHAPTER 29

So we county workers who drank coffee, smoked, ate sugar-laden goodies, and got together for happy hour were exposed to all sorts of addicts and addictions. The substances might be different, and the people abusing them as varied as the substances, but the end results were the same. The substance drove the host it inhabited to use more and more of it, causing deteriorating health as well as relationships. Addiction is addiction is addiction, to gambling, nicotine, alcohol, abusive relationships, crack, meth, heroin, and opium. Quite a few Southeast Asian refugees arrived here addicted to opium. In the golden triangle, Myanmar, Thailand, and Laos, they were opium farmers. Some smoked part of their crops, using it as medicine to dull pain, to quell hunger, and to dream.

One morning I found myself standing next to a hospital bed incongruously placed in a shack in San Pablo. In the bed was an emaciated opium addict who had recently suffered a heart attack. Now he was extremely weak and almost totally bed-bound. Both he and his wife were addicts in the process of detoxification, and because of this she was in no state to help him with his activities of daily living, like getting out of bed to bathe and use the toilet, or just helping him to sit up in bed. Relatives in Laos had been sending them opium, but not enough to sustain their habits. Watching their parents using general assistance money to buy drugs, their children were fed up and on the verge of throwing them into the streets, a desperate act in a culture where elders are respected and cared for by their children.

The couple lived in a room consisting of nothing but the hospital bed, mattresses on the floor, a few low, straw stools, and a sewing machine set on a plank supported by bricks. The toilet and shower extended off the room alongside an area for the kitchen, which consisted of one counter, a sink, and two gas burners. I did not see a fridge. They shared this space with their daughter, her husband, and their two children.

Every time I went, a constant stream of people flowed through. Whether they were visiting or also lived there, I never knew. The daughter was always seated on a low stool in front of the sewing machine. Women of different ages squatted on either side of her. One of them cut pieces of fuzzy material, a front and a back, from a pattern laid out on the floor. The machine whirred constantly as the daughter stitched these pieces together, then passed them to the woman sitting to her right. This woman stuffed the emerging teddy bear's body with cotton batting, which she pulled out of a large burlap bag. When she completed her task, she handed the body to yet another woman, who stitched on buttons for the eyes and nose. They worked continuously, as a large mound of now cute little teddies grew higher and higher. Sometimes they worked in silence, sometimes they chatted animatedly. When the parents just lay around, they occasionally appeared angry and sullen. Their singsong voices rose and fell in the tiny, stuffy room. In broken English, one of the women told me they worked for a manufacturer who paid them a few cents for each bear.

On one of my visits, all was a-hustle and bustle. The sewers sewed, children ran in and out of the house. The father, somewhat more lively, I was happy to notice, was sitting up on the edge of the hospital bed. His wife had completed the detox program and had gained weight. Flesh padded her previously skeletal frame, and she looked quite youthful. A tiny spark twinkled in her previously dull eyes.

It was a hot day. Fuzzy fibers of cotton batting, the whirr of the sewing machine, and the voices of the women and children filled the small room. Suddenly, while I was showing the wife how to assist her husband to a seat at the side of the bed, the familiar, unloved smell of squashed stinkbug assailed me. When

I had first entered the room I'd noticed people squatting in the kitchen, busily chopping vegetables on wooden boards on the floor, but I hadn't looked closely. Sniffing like a bloodhound, I now looked in their direction. I saw a woman silhouetted by the sun with an embroidered scarf wrapped around her head, squatting in front of a chopping board. A cleaver shone in her right hand as she chopped large bunches of fresh cilantro. I hate cilantro. Its soapy, pungent odor reminds me of the stinkbugs I sometimes touched accidentally while climbing the large mulberry tree in our back garden in South Africa. When touched or squashed, they emit a dreadful odor, a mixture of soap, dead insects, and rot, difficult to scrub off. But yet another smell overpowered that of the cilantro. What was it? I was horrified as my gaze fell upon an enormous skinned pig lying full-length on its side, head and all. Its eyes were closed and mine closed also as I felt the room swirl around me. I sat on the floor and leaned over, allowing blood to rush to my head. I did not want to pass out in front of everyone.

The family, I was told by a young child who was gazing at me inquisitively, was preparing a lavish get-well meal for their parents. There lay the pig, only to become pork after it would be cooked slowly in the ground outside.

My Jewishness flashed to the fore. "Oh goodness, no wonder there is an injunction against eating pork." By now the smell of human sweat, material fibers, dust, fresh pig, and cilantro had combined to make me feel quite woozy. I felt the bitter taste of bile rising into my throat.

A man in a beret smiled and invited me to join the feast later that afternoon. Thank goodness I had the legitimate excuse of work. I left as quickly and as elegantly as I could, then threw up in a creek near their shack.

. . .

A new type of heroin hit the streets. It came from Mexico and was called black tar heroin. We learned about it at an in-service training session over lunch. Apparently the site in which it was injected could easily become infected and then, like a hungry monster, it would devour the surrounding flesh and muscles. Looking at the slides of infected limbs and other body parts certainly took away my appetite that day. I admired the other health-care workers who could comfortably sit and eat, sinking their teeth into glazed doughnuts while looking at revolting slides of black scarred flesh and pus, and discuss the gory details of wound dressings and infections.

Later, I was in an unfamiliar area of Pacheco, looking for the home of a new patient. I was tired. It had been another long day and it was not yet over. Apparently she skin-popped heroin and had been hospitalized for an infected finger. The finger was amputated and she was sent home, infection free, but soon developed another infection that had her back in the emergency room. This time the bacteria had done so much damage her left hand had to be amputated.

The streets did not follow any logic, but eventually I parked at the side of the road and stared at what I thought must be her house. Old American cars from the sixties and seventies, well rusted and dented, were set at angles amongst the weeds and grasses of an unkempt yard. I saw half the hairy backside of a man with greasy, long, mousy hair hanging around his face as he peered into an engine. He was not wearing a shirt, and his large belly spilled over the front of his pants. He didn't even look up when I asked if Barbara lived in this house.

"Yeah," he grunted, still peering into the engine: charm itself.

The amputee, Barbara, answered the door, holding down a very large and unfriendly looking mongrel with her right hand, the remaining one.

"Come in," she said. "I'll put him outside."

I stared at her. She had straight black hair and wore a black T-shirt and shorts. She wore black flip-flops and her heels were cracked and dirty. Her right hand, too, was dirty. The undersides of her nails were black, and not from goth polish, and her face and neck appeared grimy. Her pupils almost obliterated her dark brown irises and, surrounded by the large whites of her eyes, made it look as if there were two fried eggs on her face. While we sat at a table so that I could fill in forms, one of her room- mates sauntered in. To describe her as Rubenesque would have been kind. Her brown hair fell in strings down her broad back. A white T-shirt ended just above her hips, and that was it; there was no more clothing to her ensemble. She carried a bottle of Jack Daniels in her hand, nodded in our direction, and brought it to her mouth, slugging it down. From elsewhere in the home, the sweet smell of pot wafted our way. The amputee assured me that she was managing, and if she needed help with, for instance, cutting bread or bathing, this Jack Daniels–swigging friend was "at hand," so to speak.

After I left I called her doctor to inform him that as of now her wound looked clean and the stump was healing well, and I was sure she would have no trouble using her right hand for skin-popping, her activity-of-daily-living of choice.

CHAPTER 30

At least Nancy and Barbara didn't have children. The only
people they hurt were themselves, and of course neither of
them had health insurance, so they were covered by Medi-Cal.
Addicts exist in order to fulfill their cravings; all else goes by
the wayside. Many of them get pregnant and don't even know
it. Their children are born drug-addicted and raised in foster
homes or by family members. Children need to eat, to be loved,
to be secure, to go to school, and to be enjoyed. These needs
are too much for addicts, and so their children are neglected and
abandoned. A grandmother told me about visiting her daughter
and grandchildren in Texas, where she found the children alone
and starving, with sores on their bodies and runny noses. The
oldest son had managed to hustle about fifty dollars and given it
to his mother to buy them food. She had taken the money, gone
out, and never returned. Now the grandmother had these children and was trying to make up for all they had never had. The
oldest son, obviously in a deep depression, stayed home all day,
barely moving and barely eating. When he did respond to questions it was obvious he was a sensitive, intelligent boy, his young
life in ruins because of his mother's addictions.

I read the new referral on my desk and remembered the article I had read in the Sunday edition of the *San Francisco Chronicle*
a month before. It was about assaults on three different prostitutes in the Tenderloin area of San Francisco. One, apparently
from an upper-class family on the Peninsula, was found battered
to death. Not too long afterward, the next, from Marin County,
was discovered in a coma after having suffered a severe beating.
These two women were both white and in their late twenties.
Each had a son, and each was a drug addict. A third woman, a

juvenile, had been found unconscious with a gunshot wound to her neck. She was in San Francisco General. Because of her status as a minor, nothing else was written about her.

The referral on my desk was to a "female, GSW (gunshot wound) to neck at C2 and C3, living with grandmother. CPS (Child Protective Services) removed juvenile from mother." I looked at her age and was horrified to see she was born in 1980. She was fifteen years old.

My supervisor told me that she was a prostitute who had been found in an alleyway in San Francisco.

"Oh yes, I read an article about prostitutes in the Sunday paper about a month ago. I'm sure that's her—how many young prostitutes can there be, especially those who have been shot in the neck?"

She now lived with her grandmother in Pacheco. The family did not have a phone, and the nurse told the grandmother I would be coming later that day.

I drove along Highway 4 toward Pacheco. The first rains had begun. The gentle, rolling, tawny hills, which reminded me of the curves of lionesses' backs lying in the veld, were beginning to turn a tentative green, as if an artist were trying out a new color. Dark green trees and woody areas cascaded downward into valleys.

My thoughts were on the patient, a prostitute at fifteen years old. My first kiss was at that age, but the physical act of intimacy did not even occur to me. In the closely knit, mostly Jewish South African world in which I grew up, sex so young was not an issue. As for prostitution…

I parked outside a small home. The place I was looking for was a shed in the backyard. I knocked on the door and a middle-aged woman with graying hair and a cigarette in her hand opened it. The room behind her was dark. She peered at me, squinting into the sunlight.

"Hi," I introduced myself.

"Come on in, we was expecting you," she said in a deep voice well seasoned by cigarettes.

I walked into a tiny room. The shades and curtains were drawn, so I waited for my eyes to grow accustomed to the dark. I saw a door and, thinking the patient would be in the other room, stepped toward it. "Don't go in there," said the grandmother. "My husband's sleeping."

I wondered where the patient could be. Hearing a "hi," I turned around to see a sweet-looking young woman sitting on a torn and faded loveseat.

"Oh my goodness," I said. "Are you Marlene? I thought you'd be in a hospital bed at the very least. Weren't you shot really high in your neck?"

She nodded, looking proud, smiled, and patted a cushion next to her. "Sit here."

She was cute, petite, and like all the kids her age, she wore huge baggy jeans and an oversize flannel shirt. Her shiny brown hair, parted down the middle, fell straight to her shoulders. Lovely, deep blue, Asian-looking eyes, framed by long, black lashes, enhanced high cheekbones, a small, perky nose, and full lips. Her white skin shone as if it had been polished to perfection.

This is a prostitute? I thought. This sweet young thing? I felt like putting my arms around her to protect her from further harm, knowing at the same time that she was well versed in the ways of the streets but had not been smart enough to prevent herself from nearly being killed.

We sat on the lumpy loveseat. Next to it stood a TV, on top of which were framed photographs. One was of a pretty young woman with long, straight, brown hair and large, deep blue eyes. At first I thought it was Marlene, but her eyes were different. Another photo showed an angelic looking boy of about nine. His complexion was bronze-gold and he had large lips and a broad nose. A halo of loose, golden curls surrounded his face.

Her grandmother remained with us in the tiny living room, sitting on a chair that had seen better days. She smoked incessantly. Every time I asked Marlene a question, her grandmother answered, turning the answer into a litany of her own medical complaints.

"Marlene, do you get headaches?" I asked.

"A few, sometimes..."

Her grandmother interrupted, "I get them all the time, really bad. I've had cancer, and I suffer from nerves. I can't sleep, just like Marlene can't either. Can you get us nerve pills?" (Mentally, I noted "drug-seeking behavior.") I explained that I could neither prescribe, nor provide, any medication.

Marlene had been shot once. The bullet entered the side of her neck between C2 and C3, grazed her spinal cord, and exited the other side. Whoever shot her left her for dead. A homeless man called an ambulance and she was taken to San Francisco General. That bullet should have rendered her a quadriplegic, on a respirator, but all she seemed to suffer was some unsteadiness when she walked. Her right arm was slightly weaker than her left arm, and her fine motor control had been affected. Her spatial judgment was slightly impaired, so that when she got up to walk she wobbled, then bumped into the loveseat and chair. Her behavior was somewhat impulsive, but then it probably had always been so.

After finishing the evaluation I told them I would come twice a week for three weeks, then once a week for two weeks. We would work on improving Marlene's cognition, balance, and fine motor control. We agreed upon days and times. This was important, because I had no way of contacting them. Before I left, the grandmother again asked me to speak to a doctor about nerve and sleeping pills. Again I explained she would have to see a doctor herself.

During one of our sessions I had Marlene draw pictures to improve her fine motor control. She handed me a completed picture, a childlike rendering of a one-story box house surrounded by a picket fence. An orderly row of flowers stood at attention on either side of the path leading to the house. There were no people in the picture.

"Is that the kind of house you'd like to live in?"

"Yeah."

"Have you lived in a house like that?"

"One time, when my mom went to prison for two years. I was nearly eleven and I went to live with my aunt, Mom's sister, in Washington State. She and her husband lived in a house like that. There was a big tree outside my room. They are born-again Christians, and her husband beat me if I didn't do well in school, or when I was sent home from school for doing things, you know..."

Reaching upward, she brought down the pictures from the top of the TV, along with a pile of others which were not framed, but lying alongside. She pointed to the pretty woman. "That's my mom, you'll meet her, she's gonna come here. I was living with her when this shooting happened. I hadn't come home for a few days, and she said she was thinking of calling the police when they came to tell her I'd been shot and was in San Francisco General Hospital. She told me she came there and pinched me, and I shouted, and she was glad because she knew that I could feel."

"How did they know her address?"

"I was in a coma when they brought me in. They said I was butt naked, and of course there was no ID, so they called me Jane Doe. The nurse told me that after twenty-four hours I sat up and opened my eyes. They asked who I was, and I told them and gave them my address. I don't remember any of what happened. The police want me to remember, because maybe I can help them find out what happened to the other women. I'm the only one who survived.

"Anyway, I have an older sister. I don't have a picture of her. She taught me to knit—she learned it in juvenile hall. But her and I, we fight. She's a mom now, she's seventeen."

She flipped through the pictures and showed me one of a tow-haired young boy, freckles spread like pepper flakes on his little nose. His blue eyes were surrounded by the same thick, black lashes they all shared.

"That's my brother, we call him Andy. He's in a foster home. My mom said we can go and see him soon and tell him what happened to me."

Then she brought down the picture of the bronze angel. "That was my older brother. We were really close, always. I know that he saved me when I was shot. The only thing I remember about the whole thing is that I saw him flying through the air and I felt him putting his hands around my neck to save me. He knew what was happening."

"Where is he now?"

"He's dead. One of my mom's boyfriends hanged him because he said he was a half-breed. He hanged him in a tree near our house. I came home and saw him hanging. That happened a few years ago. I was nine."

She told me this without any change in her expression, then immediately continued. "You remember seeing my little brother two days ago?"

Indeed I had. During our session he'd come barreling into the home, a sturdy fellow of about four years old who was being chased by a tall man with a belt in his hand. The man was lean with jet black hair, chiseled cheekbones, an aquiline nose, and brown eyes. "Cruel" is the best word to describe his appearance. If I'd seen him on the street at night I would have crossed to the other side, fast. Apparently he was not allowed in the house, because he stopped at the door and did not go any further. He nodded at us and disappeared. Marlene told me he is her mom's boyfriend.

The following week Marlene and I stood in the poorly lit bathroom. She had improved quickly and was now able to attempt her main goal, to apply makeup. After studying herself awhile, she shook a bottle of foundation, poured some into the palm of her hand, and applied it under her eyes, then smoothed the remainder onto her porcelain skin.

"Why under your eyes?"

"'Cause of the shadows."

"Marlene," I said. "You want to see shadows? Look at my eyes."

She scrutinized me.

"Not so bad, I'll look worse than that when I'm your age."

"Just how old do you think I am?"

"Twenty-eight," she replied.

I laughed, but I was thinking she probably thought no one lived to be over thirty. I was forty-eight. That same afternoon, I met her mom and understood why Marlene so misjudged my age. Her mom was probably in her mid-thirties, but the attractive face in the photo was now sallow, deeply lined, and haggard. The pupils were pinpricks in eyes that resembled opaque buttons on a torn rag doll. Her face was a testament to the life of a prostitute and drug addict—not a good career advertisement. She stroked Marlene's hair with her nicotine-stained fingers as her daughter continued applying makeup. Marlene's hand trembled ever so slightly when she applied the liquid eyeliner in a thick line above her upper lids. Then came layers of mascara, a heavy dose of blush, dark lip liner, and lipstick. She pulled her hair back and knotted it on top of her head. No longer was she a sweet young thing.

"You're so pretty, you don't need that makeup," said her mom, a cigarette drooping out of the corner of her mouth. Like her daughter, she wore baggy jeans and a large flannel shirt.

She stayed with us that afternoon and displayed an active interest in Marlene's treatment. Marlene and her mom bantered, playfully hitting each other, imitating the people on *The Jerry Springer Show.*

From then on, her mother visited during treatments. The grandmother also sat with us, always talking about her aches and pains but sometimes joining in the banter. Occasionally I saw Mom's boyfriend in the street, but he never came inside.

Marlene and I sat alone one day, playing a card game. She pulled out more photos and held them up for me to see. The first was of two heavily muscled teenagers. Tattoos covered their pumped-up biceps and deltoids.

I looked again, and gasped. I had worked with the younger one, who had been paralyzed in a shooting. His mother had shown me this same photo while saying, "Look at my baby, look at him now, so thin, no muscles. He was shot in a drive-by shooting." I had doubted her story; no one is shot in the abdomen nine times at close range in a drive-by. Come to think of it, his mom and Marlene's looked alike. They both lived in the same area. What a strange small world, I thought.

Marlene noticed my gasp. "You know him? That's my cousin. He was also shot, a while ago. He is paralyzed from the waist down, but you know, he just came out of jail again and he's so happy, because he said he can get a hard-on."

Marlene responded well to treatment. She had met all of her goals, and it was time for me to leave. The agency arranged for her to have a tutor and referred her to an outpatient clinic. I gave her mom the information. She took the pieces of paper with names and phone numbers from me, folded them into the pocket of her flannel shirt, then said she had to go out. She would be back soon. As soon as she said that, Marlene became anxious. It was the first time I had seen her like that.

"Mom," she said. "Mom, don't go. You promise you'll be back? Can I come with you? Please come back, you promise."

"Hey, Marlene?" Her mom lit a cigarette and walked to the door, then turned to look at Marlene through a cloud of smoke.

"Have I ever let you down?

CHAPTER 31

On the radio, on TV, on movies, and in literature, psychological and otherwise, families are termed "dysfunctional." Dysfunctional does not even come close to describing some of the families we see. They do not fit into any convenient mold or format we have learned about, nor do they match those we have seen revealing all on TV. In fact, the things I see make dysfunction seem the norm.

The thirty-six-year-old mother, Sally Ann, was from Tennessee, the only girl in a family of ten brothers. They were, she told me, raised in a tarpaper shack. Somehow she made her way out to the Bay Area, where she again lived in a shack, this time sheetrock. She was born with a seizure disorder and also had severe asthma which was getting worse, so she was dependent on oxygen. The first day I met her, she was sitting up in her hospital bed, oxygen cannulae in her nostrils, speaking to me in wheezing gasps. Her straight brown hair hung down in scraggly wisps. She was so pale it was difficult to distinguish her from the sheets, except for the dark shadows under her eyes.

Six years ago Sally Ann was diagnosed with multiple sclerosis. She was well known to the agency nurses, who have seen her sporadically over the years. The disease did not prevent her from bearing a daughter, against medical advice as she was incontinent and could not walk more than a few steps at a time. When I first discussed her case with the "matching" nurse, she looked up at me from beneath her autumn-palette glasses frames and referred to the daughter as "the Devil's spawn," so named by her because of Sally Ann's live-in partner, "Big Daddy." On my first visit he sat in the room adjacent to Sally Ann's, drumming his fingers on the arms of the brown easy chair in which he spent most of his time. An aura of violence surrounded him, and I felt distinctly ill at ease in his company. Over time, I learned that when he was not out drinking and drugging, he sat at home chain-smoking and drinking beer. Sometimes he was in the yard with his teenage son from a former liaison, tinkering with the rusted cars that cluttered the tiny area. Any love left in him was lavished on his two Labradors, who lay at his feet, gazing at him lovingly, while he fondled their scruffs. He had been known to slug his common-law wife, who always had fresh or fading bruises on her arms and torso. She often sported a black eye, which she got from falling, apparently. She even got a shiner after Big Daddy visited her in the hospital. She told me she had fallen off her bed. I don't want to think what he did to their four-year-old daughter. Between sobs one afternoon, Sally Ann told me Big Daddy slept in the same bed as their daughter. Sobbing and wheezing, she said she would like her daughter to sleep in the hospital bed with her. The abuse had been reported by visiting nurses and social workers. Sally Ann had been offered several opportunities to be placed in a board and care home and to have her daughter placed in a foster home. However, each time, after initially agreeing to these offers, she wept and threatened suicide if they took her away from Big Daddy.

The disease is unrelenting, and Sally Ann became almost entirely bed-bound, although she still managed to fall and constantly sported black eyes. Sometimes she sat in bed, breathing oxygen through the nasal cannulae pipes attached to the concentrator, crying. It was hard not to feel sorry for her. On one visit she told me she had found two loaded guns that Big Daddy kept in the night drawer next to his bed. At that point I informed my supervisor I would not return to their house.

The same day she told me about the guns, I heard over my car radio that counseling was being offered to families who had problems with drugs, alcohol, violence, and sexual abuse. Fine, I thought, for those who know they are in need of counseling. Sally Ann complained, but refused help. What would happen to her daughter when Sally Ann died? How would her daughter grow up? Would her daughter grow up?

Truth, it is often said, is stranger than fiction. Three years after I said I would never go back there, a doctor requested I evaluate Sally Ann for equipment. "Just one time," said my supervisor, when I reminded her why I wouldn't go back. I added that she had all the equipment she needed, anyway.

"She did," she replied, "but their house went up in flames and everything in it burned down. They have moved to an apartment complex and she needs new equipment."

Reluctantly, I went to their new apartment. Sally Ann told me about the fire. "Daddy," she said to Mr. Charming, who was sitting in a new chair, "show her the article." He rummaged in a drawer and produced a clipping from the local newspaper—"house blew up in San Pablo. Firefighters could not go into the home because of live ammunition inside." They beamed, as much as either of them could, with something akin to pride as I read the article. Daddy had been in the neighborhood bar when, apparently, an electric circuit blew. Somehow Sally Ann dragged herself, the oxygen concentrator, and their daughter outside, and so they survived.

A year later, I was sent back yet again. Big Daddy had a heart attack and died! None of us had thought he would go first. Now I was to observe how she managed without his assistance.

"He was sitting in the chair," a gaunt and deathly pale Sally Ann told me, "when he just keeled over, out of the chair and onto the floor. I got out of bed and tried CPR, but he was gone, Big Daddy's gone, and he left me with mounds of unpaid bills." She sat upright in bed, staring at me, her face like a death mask.

Sally Ann dealt with her anxiety by freebasing. Her disability income vanished on drugs; she and her daughter had no food. Someone living upstairs gave her daughter meals. The freebasing was, for her, a way not to deal with what was happening in her life, and she was hell-bent on self-destruction. Of course I told her that this was not an ideal situation, and I would have to make a report on it. I did make my report to the authorities, but as far as I know, nothing was ever done. Probably Sally Ann lives on, and her daughter takes care of her. Maybe the authorities did remove her daughter, and maybe she is now living in a supportive environment, doing really well in school, studying family law, and maybe Sally Ann has joined Big Daddy in the sky.

CHAPTER 32

The first changes in the health-care system began in the early 1990s, in hospitals. Health insurance companies pay a certain amount per patient, based on "diagnostic related groups." For example, the total amount allotted to a hospital for the care of a woman diagnosed with breast cancer might be forty thousand dollars, irrespective of her age, other related health problems, type of cancer, and so on. Therefore the hospital, in order to make a profit, is inclined not to order too many tests, and only to provide the minimum amount of care: if they exceed the limit, they lose money. By not making use of all available treatments and therapies, the hospital profits.

Because hospital stays became shorter, people were sent home who still needed skilled care, and so home health agencies began seeing a great number of people who were still very ill. It can be beneficial for patients to be in their home environments, but patients now needed more skilled nursing and therapist visits than before. It was the insurance companies who dictated the amount of care patients received—not doctors or nurses, who understood the patients and the nature of their diseases, but cost-saving accountants. Apparently, insurance companies do not understand the laws of cause and effect. Their next step was to investigate the possibilities of defraying Medicare and Medi-Cal costs for home health.

I was hired in 1992 into a place of work declared by my supervisor to be as secure as that of a chrysalis in the dark comfort of its self-made cocoon.

Within the next few months, my position as a therapist in home health for the county became extremely insecure. When I first began, the county was flush with money and was, apparently, absolutely dedicated to the health, safety, and well-being of its citizens. When the county, along with the rest of California and, indeed, America, began its plummet deep down the tunnel of not-enough-money and slid into a recession, budget cuts began. Essential services were cut or downsized, along with mental health facilities, libraries, drug and alcohol rehabilitation programs, fire departments, and after-school activities—in short, the services which hold together the fragile veneer of civilization. One of the more draconian requirements in the new guidelines we received on a daily basis from Medicare and Medi-Cal was that patients were, from now on, to be referred to as "consumers." That change in wording caused a shift in the attitudes of health-care workers, who now became providers in the health-care industry. The people we treated, who had previously suffered from illness or disabilities, were seen as vampiric entities who sucked up or consumed as many "services" as they could get away with.

For the next five years we were told in our weekly staff meetings, and in a never-ending onslaught of newsletters, that there would be changes and cuts in home health care. Of course this made me doubt the rosy future I had been promised, and it did not create a feeling of ease and security for anyone. Growing up in South Africa had not engendered feelings of security about my own future, or anybody else's, for that matter. I remember always knowing that circumstances would change, whether from "die swart gevaar" or the worsening system of apartheid. One way or another, as whites, our future was neither certain nor secure. Going to Israel only consolidated these beliefs. There, after all, my being married and pregnant was not enough to ensure a safe life. Everything was swept away. Ever since, I have lived my life as if edging along a craggy, razorlike ridge: just one wrong step, at any time, and all could come tumbling down.

My newfound cocoon dissolved before I had enough time to bask in its protective warmth and softness. The nursing supervisor began labeling consumers as being "manipulative." Why, she asked me, did I request a hospital bed for a young man dying of liver cancer? Hadn't he managed without a bed up to now? Couldn't I see he was "manipulating the system?"

The nurse in charge of his case and I walked behind the supervisor as she shuffled to her desk to review our notes. We listened to her haranguing about someone she had never seen. We explained that both of us, on separate visits, found a gaunt man, desperately ill, unable to move without assistance from someone else. He was stretched out on the sofa in the living room. We had both seen red spots on his heels, his emaciated buttocks, and his shoulder blades, the ominous beginnings of pressure sores. His wife, who until now had helped him, along with caring for their four children, had collapsed from exhaustion and stress, and she herself was in the hospital. I almost had to beg for permission to order a hospital bed, urgently. On the day it was delivered, he died. What a shame, the delivery company had been manipulated into sending a bed to someone who no longer required it—what a waste of time and money.

At first it appeared that the layoffs were affecting the nurses only. Because Medicare decreased their reimbursement for home health care, the county's share of the agency's costs rose significantly. In nonstop memos, we read that the county contribution to the home health agency needed to be reduced. The first step would be to move public health nurses from the agency and place them in other public health programs, according to seniority; then the registered nurses (RNs); then the licensed vocational nurses (LVNs). The rationale was that the amount of money paid in salaries would be less, but it was difficult for us to believe this would really happen, as the nurses seemed to be essential to the agency. However, it really did happen: one day, someone was there—someone who had been there for as long as I could remember; then, poof, they were gone.

According to our supervisor, the doctor in charge of the Public Health department was totally dedicated to serving the poor and the needy, and believed in rehabilitation. She didn't think the "bean counters" were watching us therapists, especially as most of us only worked part time and we did not earn the same salaries as the nurses did. For a while our positions seemed fairly safe, but it was deeply disturbing to me to see all that was changing and shifting around us.

As providers in the health-care "industry," we were required to increase productivity so that the industry would be profitable. New regulations began, and the rehabilitation workers were required to see 4.5 patients a day. This standard had to be kept even though we drove long distances from one home to another. We were allowed only half an hour for follow-up visits, as opposed to the hour we'd had previously, no matter the state of the so-called consumer.

CHAPTER 33

This particular day began awry. Either my not-very-shrill alarm did not ring, or I hadn't heard it. I woke up feeling like I still needed four more hours to sleep, but I forced my eyes open to look at the clock: 8:15. Oh dear God, I start work at 8:30. In all my years of working I had never been late, and that includes my years of rising at the ridiculous hour of 3:30 a.m. on the kibbutz, to be ready for the trucks to take us to the melon fields.

I flew to my kitchen, turned on the gas to heat the water for my absolutely necessary cup of coffee, and flew back up the eight stairs to the shower. Pulling on my pants and T-shirt, I wondered why the kettle was not yet whistling. I ran down the stairs and to my dismay discovered I had turned the gas on, but in my haste did not even notice that the kettle was not on the burner. Cursing at myself, I placed the kettle on the correct burner and finished dressing. As soon as the water boiled I poured it into the coffee filter I had placed on my car mug, then turned around to grab an apple. Reaching for the mug I saw a brown stain spreading across the burner and oven top. I had poured in too much water. Angrily I placed the cover on the mug, grabbed my handbag and beeper, and flew into the car.

8:40 a.m. Halfway out of the driveway I realized I'd left the mug inside, but it was now too late to retrieve it. I would have to make do without coffee. In the office I found three messages on my desk, one from a doctor whom I had been trying to contact for a week. I knew I would have difficulty getting hold of him again, and I needed to speak to him, to get his okay for equipment and visits for a patient with full-blown AIDS. The other two messages were from parents of the babies I was supposed to see that day. The children were sick and the parents had, correctly, cancelled my visits. However, this meant I wouldn't be able to see the required five patients. My statistics would be low, I would lose my job, the agency would close, the patients would all die horrible deaths.

These were my spiraling depressive thoughts as I tried to contact another patient, but her phone just rang and rang. As I counted the rings (for documentation purposes), a nurse placed two new referrals on my desk.

One was to a patient, Linda, with bilateral calcaneal (ankle) fractures and a compression fracture between two lumbar vertebrae, L4 and L5. Apparently she had jumped out of the fourth-floor window of the county jail because she didn't want to detox from heroin. Instead of dying, she now had fractured ankles, was non-weight-bearing, and had to detox anyway. Other than Tylenol, she was not allowed painkillers, because of her history of addiction. The referral stated that she lived in a trailer park and didn't have a phone, so I would have to go unannounced.

The nurse who made the referral was a space cadet whose outlook remained frozen in the years she was a flower child. She always floated into the office with a beatific grin on her face, as if all were perfect in this best of all possible worlds. Like parachutes, her skirts billowed 'round her ankles in shades of vivid blue, purple, orange, red, and green. Long strings of beads complemented each outfit, twirling around her neck. Sometimes I felt like yanking on those beads to anchor her to the earth. Her idea of healing was to tell patients to meditate on light and love—which, in itself, is not a bad idea, but not always practical either. Once she told a desperately poor, morbidly obese woman with severe depression, congestive heart failure, and diabetes to buy and care for a plant. When I saw the patient a week later, the plant had withered and died, leaving the patient even more depressed.

The nursing supervisor saw my expression when I went to her desk and pointed to the nurse's name.

"I know," she said, rolling her eyes. "The other nurses are out seeing clients, I had to send her."

Before I left for the trailer park I bought a tepid cup of coffee from the Afghani man who sold snack food from a van in the parking lot. Against my better judgment, I followed the nurse's directions and soon found myself in a dead-end street. I made a U-turn and went left, right, left again, until I realized I was now officially lost. I was also hot and irritable. Eventually I found my way to the part of Rumrill Road that goes through what I think of as the Bible Belt of San Pablo, a stretch of the road lined with small concrete churches, some without windows. The names are mostly handwritten on boards or doors: Iglesia Arca de Noe; Bibleway Missionary Church; Iglesia Mision Emanuel A.D.; Renewed Hope Church of the Living Christ, Our Motto:...making ready a people prepared for the Lord (Luke 1:17).

In fact, there is even a Holy Hands Beauty Salon.

I could not find the number of the particular trailer park I was looking for. Eventually, after driving behind monster trucks whizzing west, and cars bearing bumper stickers stating "Fill the Air with Prayer," "God Lives, He Forgives," and one I needed as my mantra, "I'm Too Blessed to Be Stressed," I saw the number on a wooden gate. Hallelujah, the Bible Belt prayers had worked! I parked on the side of the road and walked into the park. Rusty campers and trailers were lined haphazardly alongside each other. Numbers were painted onto the asphalt in front of the trailers. I looked for number 16. I found 15, 17, 14, but no number 16. Logic told me it should be in the vicinity of 15, 17, 13, 14, but it wasn't. A large Rottweiler looked at me as he paced back and forth behind an iron fence like a lion in a cage. He bared his teeth and barked, looking like the hound of the Baskervilles. "Oh Lord," I prayed, still under the influence of so many churches, "help me." Just as I finished this short plea, an elderly lady behind the wheel of an old Buick drove into the park.

She slowed down when she saw me waving my hand in her direction. "Where's number 16?" I asked her.

"Sorry, honey, I don't know, follow me. I'm going to my daughter, she used to be the manager, she'll know." I walked behind her until she stopped outside a trailer. A pimply-faced, mousy blonde with rotten teeth stood outside holding the hand of a little boy, who jumped with glee when he saw the car: "Granny, Granny!" The woman driving greeted him with a hug, then asked her daughter where number 16 was. The daughter opened the car's back door, shoved her kid inside, and shrugged, "I don't know." Her mother apologized as they drove away, leaving me wandering between the trailers, gingerly stepping around large piles of dog shit. The hound of the Baskervilles was obviously not the only dog in the park.

Finally, between numbers 42 and 22, I saw the number 16 painted on the asphalt. I climbed up four rickety wooden steps and banged on the trailer door. A disheveled, gray-haired, bespectacled man opened the door and beckoned me in. He sort of smiled, displaying decaying, dirty yellow teeth. Linda lay on a hospital bed. Behind it was a relic of a chair, covered with stained blankets and sheets. The air was stuffy, the carpet under-neath stuck to my shoes. A commode was placed next to the bed. I was thankful that someone had poured out the contents. My eyes began to itch. "Cats," I thought. "There are cats here somewhere."

"Can I sit?" I asked. They both nodded but did not indicate anyplace. I pushed the sheets aside on the chair and sat on the very edge, careful not to sink back into goodness only knew what.

"Where did you park?" asked the man.

"On the street," I wheezed.

"This is not a good neighborhood. Next time come around and park in our spot—we don't have cars."

"Do you have cats?" I asked, eyes watering, nose twitching.

"Five."

Wheezing, I explained I was allergic. Obligingly, the man opened the door and whistled, and what looked like a flock of cats flew from a back room to the outside.

Linda was large, but not excessively so. She was in her early forties, but like most drug addicts who spend their time on the streets, she looked much older. Her salt-and-pepper hair hung down in rats' tails. She wore a flannel shirt and navy shorts. Casts covered her legs from her knees down to her feet. Her eyes watered, and she licked her lips constantly. She did not have any teeth that I could see, and her lined cheeks sunk in around her gums.

"I'm her ex-husband," said the man. "I don't live here, but I've come around to help the old bag. When will she get Medi-Cal? She has to get to a methadone clinic. I can't stand to see her like this. We don't have any money. When the first of the month comes I can help her, but that's four days away. She doesn't have pills. They sent the wrong wheelchair. You've got to do something. She has a doctor's appointment at the hospital today. How are we going to get there?"

Shut up, I thought. Stop your barrage and let her speak. Just shut the fuck up. Open the window, I can't breathe. Why didn't you make arrangements to get to the hospital? What the hell can I do about it?

This is what I thought, not what I said.

I turned to the woman and asked how she got to the commode, how she bathed and dressed. Was she eating?

Although I was curious, I decided against asking why she had been in jail. It is not one of the questions on our evaluation forms, but curiosity often gets the better of me. When I ask, I am told: robbery, assault, rape, murder. Sometimes it is better not to know.

Linda began complaining, echoing the man. "The wheelchair is uncomfortable, it don't feel right, I need more painkillers, food..." The man began crying. "Old bag," he sniffled, wiping his nose with his sleeve, "it'll be okay." He patted her hand. "Things have been worse." He leaned over to kiss her, and tears welled up in her eyes and fell down her sunken cheeks.

He turned to me. "We have to get to the methadone clinic. I'm on methadone, it will help her." Suddenly he became angry. "I can't stand to see her suffering. What are you going to do?"

Just then the woman shifted and I saw what looked like a
syringe between the folds of the blanket. I ignored it.

"Did you apply for Medi-Cal while you were in the hospital?"
I asked.

"Yes."

"Okay, it will come through, it takes time, at least a couple of
weeks."

Don't you know there are hundreds of others applying? You
aren't the only ones in the world in a bad situation. You've been
on heroin for years. You chose to be on the drugs. You got in
this mess. You tried to kill yourself rather than go cold turkey.
I'm sick of all of you, fucking yourselves and other people up
and then demanding things, like the world owes you something.
Do you know how much money is spent on you? You've already
had two operations. You've also got hepatitis C and B, and high
blood pressure. You'll need more hospitalizations, medications,
and care. You'll eventually be a candidate for a liver transplant.
Who do you think is paying for this? I know you had children,
where are they now? Were they born addicted to drugs? Did
they have to suffer the pangs of withdrawal? Foster homes? A
bleak future?

Again, I merely thought these things as I sat with this charming couple.

Oh dear, this was no good. My compassion had flown out of
the windows of this filthy, cat-infested trailer. I wanted to be in
Nordstrom, looking at fine gold jewelry glistening under glass.
I wanted to feel the velvet softness of cashmere sweaters neatly
folded and laid out in jewel-rich colors.

I shook my head to clear it of these thoughts and asked her
to show me how she got to the commode—heaven forbid she
breaks something else just trying to move from her bed to the
toilet or sink. She used her hands to push on the rails of the
hospital bed and scoot herself over. She was able to wash from
a pail set up next to the bed. She could dress herself. There was
nothing for me to do, especially as she was in casts.

I checked her wheelchair. The medical supply company had sent the wrong chair. She needed a chair with elevating leg rests so that her casts would not scrape on the floor and the swelling in her legs and feet could go down. That meant I would have to go back to the office to find out exactly what had been ordered for her when she was discharged from the hospital, and then I would have to call the supply company and arrange for them to exchange the chair. This was frustrating because I had told the health-care plan any number of times not to use that particular supply company, because we always had problems with them. Did they listen to me? No, they didn't. Every time I told them there was an error with the equipment, they sounded totally surprised. I still had three more patients to see. Just arranging for the correct wheelchair could take hours, if not days.

"Okay," I muttered to myself, "now transport." Using my cellular phone, I called the office to find out whether transport had been arranged for Linda's appointment.

"No," said the nurse, "she should have arranged it herself on her last appointment. Why didn't she? I don't know what can be done."

By now I was grinding my teeth. "Please try," I begged. "There is no phone here and my battery is low. Could you call me back?"

"If I can arrange something," growled the nurse, who was also having a difficult day.

Linda shifted around in bed. Her eyes watered, she licked her lips, then resumed crying. The man joined in again.

"Did you want to die?" I asked her, referring to her jump out of the jail windows.

"I don't want to live if I have to go cold turkey," she said. "I've tried it before."

"Your Medi-Cal papers will come through, it takes a while. I will exchange your wheelchair. Until you are weight-bearing, I won't come back. When the casts are removed, you will need more assistance, as well as physical therapy, so I will come back and check on you then."

My phone rang. I fumbled for it in my coat pocket. The nurse had managed to arrange transport. A cab would come for her at 2:30 p.m.

I relayed this to Linda and explained that she needed to arrange transport for her next visit today, while she was at the hospital.

"Methadone," repeated the man. Suddenly he turned and looked at me carefully. "Hey, I know you, your accent. Didn't you come and help my pal Jimmy Cleveland? He had AIDS. I know you from somewhere."

I do remember faces, but I didn't remember him, nor could I recall anyone by the name of Jimmy Cleveland. I would never have forgotten the trailer park, but maybe I had lost some of my faculties.

"I'll check," I said, feeling compelled to make polite conversation. "If you are right, I'll let you know."

I handed them my card and left.

My car and everything in it was fine, and I wanted out.

Onward, but first I needed to return to the office to scrub my hands and arms, because the sanitizer I normally use did not feel sufficient. I would have liked to boil my clothes in lye as well.

After a thorough cleansing I returned to the cubbyhole I shared with the physical therapist and a social worker. The social worker sat at his desk, holding his phone with one hand and writing with the other.

"Hey," I greeted him when he hung up. "How are you? I'm having a Nordstrom kind of day," I said to him.

"A what?"

I explained my desire to work with unnecessary costly items in an atmosphere of fluorescent, controlled luxury.

"You'd hate it, I'm telling you," he said. "Those people are picky, fussy, and ungrateful."

"Who is grateful, anyway? At least there it is clean."

Sighing, I picked up the phone and called in messages about the wheelchair. I then checked my previous files. I had never worked with a Jimmy Cleveland, my mind had not left me.

I called to make sure the next patient was home. Yes, said his foster mom, he was there. I had only seen him once, but I was already head over heels in love with the six-month-old boy who had been abandoned in the hospital. He was born prematurely, addicted to cocaine and opiates. When I first saw him he was lying in a crib in the foster home, a tiny thing, the size of a two-month-old rather than a six-month-old, with lots of soft curly hair, velvet brown eyes, and long eyelashes. He had looked at me with those enormous eyes and smiled, and I melted.

Excitedly, I drove to the home. He lay on his back in his crib, watching a colorful mobile whirl overhead. I picked him up. He was as light as a feather, and the upper half of his body was stiff as a board. I stroked his back and held him close, trying to loosen his tiny, retracted shoulder blades, pulled together alongside his spine like tiny wings too afraid to unfold. His arms were flexed at the elbows, and both of his thumbs were hidden under tightly clenched fingers. His foster mother told me he looked like an alien when she first saw him, tiny and skinny. His skin had been dark purple and stretched tightly over his face. His biological mother abandoned him immediately after giving birth. Alone, in the hospital, on a respirator, he suffered the pangs of withdrawal. He also had a heart murmur. Now, containing him in my arms, I felt his limbs tremble occasionally, and his movements were jerky. Holding this innocent little boy, I felt like a lioness protecting my cub. I no longer thought of Nordstrom; "murderous" would better describe my feelings, a homicidal fury directed toward all the drug-using parents of the innocent unborn.

After fifty minutes he relaxed, his limbs loosened, and his movements became fluid, for now at least.

I had to move on. The bumper sticker on the car in front of me read, "Planned Parenthood Kills over 132,000 Children a Year." I glared at the driver as I overtook him. In my car I jabbed at the radio dial. Classical music, nope, I was not in the mood. KPFA, Berkeley's left-leaning station? Too sanctimonious. NPR had a pledge drive, again. I pulled out my tapes. The annoyingly bland, soulless cassette *Dream Spiral*? No way. The Yoga Sutras of Patanjali? Please. Did I want to learn Spanish right now? No. Back to the radio. KCBS: traffic and weather, every ten minutes. For some obscure reason, I find this station incredibly soothing, which is what I needed. The next foster home I was on my way to was not as warm and loving as the one I had just left.

I drove on, thinking of my next patient, when a car cut in front of me, causing me to swerve. Luckily, no one was in the lane next to me. I had a chance to see its bumper sticker: "Practice Random Kindness and Senseless Acts of Beauty."

The next little girl had been born with a rare genetic syndrome which causes facial and cranial malfusion of the bones. She had an enormous head, a flat forehead, and bulging eyes that did not close properly. She was blind, and she had difficulty breathing, due to the misshapen bones around her sinuses. She was always congested, and yellow mucous flowed in a never-ending stream from her nostrils. I had never met the foster mother, who worked all day and hired a babysitter, Mary, to care for the children. This was the last time I would see the child, as the foster mother and her young charges were moving out of the area.

On my first visit to the home in North Richmond, a dead rat, still bleeding, lay outside the front door. There were a few children in the home, and while I worked with the little girl I was struck by the beauty of a boy who sat in the living room with us, staring at the TV. Occasionally he glanced my way, but when he caught me looking at him he quickly turned back to the TV.

"What's your name?" I asked him.

Absolutely no response.

Mary told me his name was Demario, and he was four. He had an older brother, Sam, who also lived there. Sam went to school in the morning.

Demario never responded to my attempts to speak to him.

On subsequent visits this pattern repeated itself. Demario sat quietly watching TV. I asked what he was watching. Silence. I asked if he understood me. Silence. No response, ever. Just those melting chocolate eyes and mahogany skin, smooth and soft. I know, because I patted him sometimes when I spoke, and he didn't shift away.

Once I asked him whether he liked to look at books. As usual, he remained silent. Undeterred, I continued my one-way conversation. "Do you have books?" Nothing. "Well, Demario, I am going to buy you one." Nothing.

I looked for books in a few shops in Albany. It was hard to find something appropriate. Jimmy going fishing with his dad wouldn't do. The fruit and animals on Farmer Brown's farm would probably not be of much interest either. I could buy *The House That Crack Built*, but I didn't think it would be too helpful. Eventually I found a book about a day-care center where the teacher was African American and the six little kids formed a rainbow coalition. As I paid for it, I wondered whether Demario had ever seen a book in his short life. Had anyone ever placed him on their lap and read to him? I fantasized about taking him to a quiet place, maybe a park, near the water, where we could look at books together.

It was a while before I had a chance to give Demario the book, because the little girl had been ill and I had not visited. In fact, she was ill again today, but I told Mary I had to come to say good-bye to her and Demario.

When I got there, the babysitter was at her wit's end. The little girl was lying on the sofa. Her breath rattled in her throat and thick mucus flowed from her nostrils. Demario was at his station in front of the TV. Another child, the babysitter's hyperactive foster daughter, ran around between boxes piled high in the dark living room. Two little boys, maybe three and four years old, fought with each other. I hadn't seen them before. Apparently they had been taken in because of an emergency situation the night before. I sat on the sofa, held the little girl, who responded to my touch by smiling, and said hi to Demario, who remained silent, as usual. The other kids gathered around to inspect me.

"Demario," I called to him, "come here, I have something for you. He edged closer, but his eyes remained on the TV.

"Demario, I promised I'd bring you a book, here it is." He reached out and took the book. Immediately everyone else grabbed for it.

"It is for Demario," I said. "He will let you all look at it, but it is his." Demario handed it to the active little girl, who had reappeared from behind a box, and returned to watching TV.

Just then Sam, an older version of Demario, skipped in. He had just returned from school. All the children ran to play in the yard, except for the little girl. She could not crawl and certainly couldn't go outside.

Mary told me that Demario and Sam suffered from night terrors. Apparently Sam had been so disruptive when he began school that the bus driver did not want to pick him up. They are now both on Ritalin because they suffer from attention deficit disorder. Their suffering is caused by their mother's use of drugs.

"I could kill drug mothers," I said to Mary.

Mary was more understanding, compassionate, and kind than me. Earlier, when she had introduced me to her seven-year-old foster daughter, she'd told me the girl's biological mother is her niece, a crackhead who has several children.

"If they do drugs, they should have their tubes tied," Mary said. "Then they won't be harming anyone but themselves."

I kissed the little girl in my arms good-bye, then went to the backyard. Sam was riding a rusty tricycle on a patch of dry earth. Demario was standing on the back bar, holding onto Sam as he rode around. The other girl was chasing the two boys, who were crying. I called Demario.

"What?" he said, shocking me. This was the first word I had heard him use.

"Demario, you've been teasing me all the time, you can speak. Come here, I want to tell you something."

He approached me and I put my arm around him.

"I'm not going to see you again because you are moving away, and I can't come there, as it is too far away."

He kept quiet, but nodded, remaining snuggled under my arm.

"So, remember, the book is my gift to you."

He nodded, raised his eyes, and pointed to the book on a shelf above the refrigerator. "I took it back from the girl, I'm keeping it safe," he said.

My anger was now replaced by an overwhelming sense of futility and sadness, and my day was not yet over.

I drove to my fourth case, the second referral I had received this morning. On the way, another bumper sticker: "I Am Pro-Salmon and I Vote." What is that about, I wondered? I should not waste my precious time pondering that one, now is my time for meditation practice: take deep breaths, concentrate on my inhalations and exhalations, and get safely to the next patient. She was new to our agency, an elderly woman with terminal cancer.

A thin woman with wispy, gray hair and enormous eyes, which looked even bigger because her face was so skeletal, let me into her small, neat home.

I sunk into the soft sofa upholstered in a fabric with brown and yellow flowers on a cream background. I placed my file on the coffee table and smiled at the woman now sitting in an easy chair. Her chest rose and fell quickly as if she were desperate to suck in some air. I glanced around. A glass dining room table set for four stood in the back of the small living room. The walls were covered with photographs. A lively looking girl, her hair in braids, appeared in lots of the pictures. The woman saw me looking at the pictures.

"That's my granddaughter," she said, in a raspy voice. "I'm raising her. She's thirteen and a half now, and she goes to Berkeley High. She's a good student."

Her voice was raspy because she'd had a growth on her vocal chord removed, and some of her jawbone along with it.

I remarked that I thought she looked much better than I had imagined after I read her diagnosis.

"I was diagnosed with cancer nearly eighteen years ago. They told me I would die soon, but I couldn't up and die, because I had to raise my children. Now I have to raise my granddaughter. The Lord has blessed me."

Her needs were few. She was weak after her bout with pneumonia and wanted to know how to bathe safely and independently. I was happy to be able to help her.

After I showed her the tub bench and deep breathing exercises for energy conservation, I sat in the living room, completing my reams of paperwork. She was tired, but nevertheless gracious and patient.

Between writing I glanced up and saw a large black-and-white photo of a beautiful woman in an evening dress. She sat on a sofa, a long, light-colored tulle skirt spread out around her slender waist, like petals unfolding in the morning sun. Slender straps held the low-cut bodice on shapely shoulders. Her hair was combed back into a chignon. She was immersed in an animated conversation with three men and a woman who sat next to her. A grand piano stood behind them.

"That's me. I was beautiful," she said simply, stating the truth. Her voice betrayed no regret at having lost her looks or being disfigured from cancer.

"I owned several nightclubs in Milwaukee. During the war I had been a schoolteacher, because the men were gone fighting. After they returned, things changed, so I decided to open a nightclub. It did well, and I opened others. I managed eight of my own clubs and ran a diner."

"You must have been quite something. You still are. Here you are, alive, looking after yourself and your granddaughter. You are an inspiration."

My feelings of helplessness had now changed to gratitude for the privilege of meeting this woman whose eyes were so alive, and whose vibrant spirit radiated like a magnificent aura, transforming the very air around her, despite the ravages of cancer.

When I left her house I tuned into the classical music station. Gil Shaham played Mendelssohn's Violin Concerto in E Minor as I drove by the new bakery being built by Rubicon, a successful drug and alcohol rehabilitation treatment center which supplies cakes to stores and restaurants around the Bay Area.

There was hope, after all.

CHAPTER 34

The number of memos and newsletters about cuts and closures, together with seniority lists, increased, covering our desks like rooftops strewn across the landscape after a tornado. Did no one consider the rain forests being cut down for all this paper? I found it difficult to understand the wording of these endless memos. "This note is to keep you apprised of measures being undertaken to ensure the survivability of the HHAgency con sidering a projected 1.4 million dollar county contribution by the end of the fiscal year." The editor in me marked papers with a red pen, inserting periods and paragraphs, correcting spelling errors. Of course the only one benefiting from my proofreading efforts was me, trying to make head and tail of all of this.

The camaraderie we previously enjoyed deteriorated. Rumors flew like vultures circling above a kill. At this time everything we heard and read was still mostly in the realm of "maybe these things will happen." Those who had worked for the county for years assured us that they had similar scares every year at budget time. This year, they did concede, seemed a bit worse. Because everyone was nervous about losing their jobs, stress levels rose and hearts hardened. Workers jockeyed for what they perceived to be positions of stability.

"The agency will close."

"The agency can never shut down, it is dedicated to serving the needy."

"The home health aides will lose their jobs and won't get their retirement benefits."

"The public health nurses will lose their jobs, they *are* losing their jobs, the aides will not lose theirs."

"I'm okay, I have been with the county for a long time. Why should I worry about the person hired after me?"

"What about registered nurses? Licensed nurses? Therapists?"

"Everyone needs therapists," assured our supervisor, again, jiggling her ankle and clicking her pen. "We don't earn as much as the nurses, anyway, so our jobs are not in danger. Do you know how much nurses earn? Twice as much as we do."

It is in the best interests of a patient if workers collaborate as a team. Now, nasty words flew from one worker's mouth to the next worker's ear, without any concern for who would hear. The patients listened and reeled from the reverberations, scared that they would not have any care.

Encapsulated in bubbles of fear, no one seemed to see, or care, that when others lost their jobs those left behind would be far more pressured. No one looked beyond their personal bubbles to understand that the patients would suffer, as well as the well-being of the community. People only worried about their own tiny little worlds. We had fewer potlucks—a hint of worse things to come.

. . .

In order to cut costs by saving on rent, an office was to be closed and geographic shifts made to avoid layoffs. The Richmond office remained open, and I requested to work there, to the horror of those working in Central County. Why on earth did I want to work in those gritty neighborhoods, with those gritty people, in places that caused the Central County workers to ensure their late-model car doors were locked when they reluctantly went to see patients.

How could I explain that my commute would be far less hair-raising, and besides, I enjoyed the rich cultural mix that made up West County?

In South Africa I grew up without TV, and not because of parental concerns—there simply was no TV, period. But I read everything I could get my hands on. I sat under the mulberry tree reading about distant lands, pausing occasionally to gaze at the ever changing clouds in the endless sky and dream of adventure. In my teens I slipped into the townships where whites were forbidden to enter without a permit. These places, so very different from our gracious homes in the suburbs, were vibrant and alive, crowded, poor, dirty, scary. In winter the air was filled with smoke from open braziers, cigarette and dagga smoke, coal fires, and music, always music.

The desire for new experiences and travel must be imprinted in my DNA. Working in home health, I realized I do not need to travel far to experience the tantalizing anticipation and excitement I feel when visiting different cultures; this desire is fulfilled where I live and work. I don't have to go to Mexico or Guatemala to take Spanish immersion courses, I spend entire days immersed. Even in my car, I listen to Spanish radio stations and language cassettes. I try out my fledgling Spanish skills in the many homes I visit by speaking to the children, parents, aunts, uncles, grandparents, cousins, the endless stream, the multitudes, of family and visitors who either live in, or flow through, the homes. They simply cannot understand that I live alone, and I feel they are extremely concerned about my well-being, especially my dietary habits. They share their food with me or ply me with food to take home. I sit down to meals of nopales and chorizo, tamales, salad with chopped onion, tomatoes, and nopales, and boiled corn smeared with mayonnaise, grated white cheese, chile powder, and lemon juice, which is incredibly delicious but embeds itself in my teeth. I observe the women stirring pots of beans and steaming corn husks. One day I followed a woman to her backyard, where chickens ran around amongst the grass and the dirt. Reaching down, she grabbed one and, before I could look away, swung it by its neck—then, whoosh, sliced off its head. I gaped as I watched the headless body flap to the ground!

I jotted down home remedies, like soothing a sore throat and cough by slicing a red onion, pouring honey over the slices, and allowing it to sit overnight. The resulting juice is used as cough syrup.

Of course I watched TV with them, because the living room of every home, no matter how poor the inhabitants, is dominated by a large TV. It did not take long for me to become hooked on *Mujer, Casos de la Vida Real,* shown every morning at eleven. I scheduled visits around these telenovelas, rationalizing that it was a learning experience. If the patients could explain words and scenes I did not understand, then I knew they were functioning cognitively. A new evaluation tool.

I observed the women gathered together, especially when they prepared for ceremonies. Before a baptism or quinceañera, the women work day and night preparing decorations and gifts for guests. They wield glue guns and strips of lace, ribbon, and cloth. They fashion tortilla holders by gluing rope onto round pieces of styrofoam. They weave fabric and lace into cane baskets in which little dolls rest, nestled on padded material. Plastic gallon jugs of milk become totes decorated with layers of cloth and lace and inset with tiny pearls. Inside are party favors. Dressmakers whip up frothy concoctions of satin and lace.

Mien elders from Laos reverently bring out their beautiful, hand-embroidered heirlooms, which they had carefully placed in their closets. The women embroider the scarves they wear around their heads after marrying, and their pants, tunics, wedding clothes, even their own shrouds. The old women embroider without following a pattern, fingers flying as they form tiny cross-stitches. The older men fashion jewelry from silver—earrings, bracelets, necklaces, and amulets to be sewn on the back of wedding garments.

I attended a Mien wedding in a newly opened restaurant in San Pablo. It is situated in one of the more desolate shopping malls; besides the restaurant, there is only a laundromat and a small grocery store. The brick walls surrounding the mall are covered in red, blue, green, black, and white graffiti. Every gang appears to claim this area as their turf: the Sons of Death, the Color of Blood, Norteños, and Sureños, to name but a few.

The older guests arrived in their traditional finery. Embroidered scarves were elaborately wrapped around the women's heads. They wore hand-embroidered tunic tops over skirts. Deep, vivid pink ruffles hung around the necks of the teenagers in the bridal retinue. White sashes were tied in a specific pattern over their tunics. When the bride and groom walked, the rows upon rows of hand-worked silver pendants sewn onto the backs of their tunics tinkled gently, like a fountain. The men wore black tunics and loose-fitting pants and embroidered scarves wound around their heads. The effect was startlingly beautiful, in sharp contrast to the shabby surroundings.

The youngsters came in the oversize white shirts and baggy jeans favored by teens everywhere. Girls strutted around in high platform heels and long, slinky dresses.

Upon entering the café, I placed my gift into a large box and was handed a thimbleful of brandy. Long trestle tables were surrounded with folding chairs. I greeted the bride and groom, who twirled around so that I could inspect the silver ornaments: exquisitely wrought butterflies, fish, birds, flowers, and geometric designs, as well as bells, all crafted by the father of the groom. Women milled around the entrance of the kitchen, then entered the hall bearing trays piled high with small dishes of food. Quickly they placed the dishes on the tables and returned to the kitchen for more, a seemingly endless supply. They had risen well before dawn to prepare the food, clothe themselves, and help the young people who had never learned how to don their garments.

Some dishes set my mouth on fire and made my eyes water. Others were more subtle. I discerned sautéed bamboo shoots, daikon in hot sauces of lime juice, tomatoes, fiery peppers, slices of beef, chicken, fish. Pork, lots of pork, and piles of cilantro. I did not partake of the pork and cilantro, all too vividly remembering the feast prepared in the hot dusty shack.

At some point during the festivities the bride and groom stood up. The groom held a round tray on which stood a kettle and porcelain, thimble-sized cups. They presented their parents with tea and then began walking amongst all the guests. A Mien teen sitting behind me told me this is for luck. The guests place money in a bowl on the tray—anything, he said, from a quarter to a hundred dollars, whatever you want—and the couple serve you tea. This round took almost an hour to complete, and at the end of it they must have amassed a small fortune. Toward the end of the round a short man wearing a white shirt, a black beret, and black pants stood up and began chanting. My young interpreter told me he was the priest, or shaman. Soon all the older men gathered at a table with this priest, and they chanted for hours. My new friend told me that in Laos all the men and boys learned these prayers, but he doesn't know them.

CHAPTER 35

Despite rumors of impending disaster, loss of jobs, benefits, and self-worth, repossessed cars, mortgage foreclosures, and future homelessness, life continued, and I, like everyone else, carried on. I was referred to a woman with chronic obstructive pulmonary disease and degenerative joint disease. The person who opens a case is supposed to inform the follow-up workers if there is someone in the house or something in the surroundings that is not safe. In this instance I was, as is usually the case, given only the address and medical background.

I called her the day before. Speaking in a raspy, years-of-smoking voice, she asked me to come the next day at 8:30 a.m. Promptly the next morning, I walked up the short, cement-paved pathway and climbed the steps to a nondescript home in San Pablo. On the balcony stood flowerpots with nothing but brown sticks poking out of the soil. The floorboards on the balcony groaned and creaked when I stepped on them. I knocked on the door and waited, and waited. Silence, nothing. Again I knocked, this time a little louder. Still nothing. I knocked a third time and heard someone cough, and then the sound of footsteps became louder. Someone opened the door an inch or so.

"Hi," I said, unable to see inside. "I'm the therapist."

The door opened just a tad more and a pair of icy blue eyes stared at me, giving me chills, from the acne-scarred face of a tall man with light, curly, close-cut hair.

"Yeah," he said, "what do you want here?"

"I called yesterday, I have come to see ———."

His expression, hard and flinty, did not change, but he did open the door and bark at his mother. He let me into a home that smelled of old and fresh cigarette smoke, burned coffee, and the greasy remains of last night's dinner. His mother, an older version of him, lay on a bed in an adjacent room, smoking—obviously something she should not be doing. She beckoned me in. He shadowed me and remained leaning against the doorjamb, chain-smoking. Something about his presence caused the almost invisible hairs on my forearms to stand up. My heart felt as if it had begun training for the Olympics. My body was preparing for flight. In defiance of my body's desires, I remained in the room, asking questions and filling in my evaluation forms. I instructed the woman in energy conservation techniques and suggested that maybe, just maybe, she should not smoke so much. The man remained in the doorway, quiet and looming, throughout my visit.

Back at the office I tracked down the nurse who had made the referral. I asked her whether she had ever encountered the man who lived there.

"No," she said, "but she told me her son would be out of jail in two days."

Until I began this job I had never met so many people who knew someone in jail.

"My son is in the pen...I didn't teach him to do those things," said a grandmother as she grunted her way onto a bath bench.

"My daughter is in jail, so I'm taking care of her son. She killed his daddy," said a depressed woman. Her expression never changed as, in a monotone, she described how her daughter drove a car over her husband.

A youngish woman had a stroke because of her crack use. Dragging on a cigarette, she told me, "My doctor wrote a letter to the prison warden to let my son out of the pen, 'cause he needs to come back and take care of me."

In one home I saw a well-drafted pencil portrait of a three-year-old boy whose mom was ill. It was tacked on the wall above the boy's bed. "That is really good," I said to the chubby little fellow. "It's you, isn't it?"

"Yeah," volunteered the little boy. "My daddy's cellmate did it from a photo of me."

A two-year-old girl cried for her daddy, who had served only the first six months of a fifteen-year jail sentence. Now she is five and still cries for her daddy, who calls her once a week. She spends her weekends going to see her daddy and grandpa, who are in separate prisons.

Sometimes it seems like every home I visit is haunted by the absence of someone now imprisoned.

The statistics about people in prison bear this out. California spends more money on building prisons and warehousing inmates than it does on building schools. Sometimes I feel that the powers that be want to put the babies into prison immediately after birth and let them live out their lives there.

Unfortunately, I quite often see truly horrendous events in the course of a day's work. Because I spend a lot of time on the road, I see dreadful accidents and so many near misses that I believe there must be some beneficent agent who watches over the roads. All of these occurrences leave me decidedly shaken. For one who works in the health-care profession, I am rather squeamish. If I see someone vomiting, my guts heave in sympathy. The body fluids I hate most are those excreted from the lungs, and quite often patients collect their phlegm and mucous in glass bottles and show it to me, no doubt thinking I am a nurse and I can pass this information along to their doctor. I avert my gaze and tell them to show the nurse, as that is her job, not mine.

Because of this work in the "field," I developed a tremendous admiration for policemen, firefighters, and paramedics—for all those in the trenches, dealing on a daily basis with accidents, suffering, and violence, the not-so-beautiful side of humanity and life. How, I wondered, do they deal with the stress of their work, which is far worse than what I experience. How do they decompensate? Do they get counseling? I decided to ask, but every time I saw a policeman or policewoman, which was often, they were engaged in writing warrants, handcuffing someone, or speeding to the next situation.

One day I saw two policewomen strolling out of a Chinese restaurant. "Now is the time," I thought, hurrying to catch up with them. Tapping one on her shoulder I said, "Excuse me, but I'd like to ask some questions." The two of them were surprisingly gracious and did not seem to resent my intrusion. One told me she has to remind herself that her work is just a job. Off duty, she doesn't watch TV or read the papers. She wouldn't dream of watching *Cops*. In fact, she doesn't watch TV at all, preferring to listen to classical music.

The other woman told me she has a harder time letting go, because she lives in the same area in which she works, so almost every place she sees is a reminder of her work. Policewomen in general, they said, have an easier time dealing with stress than policemen, because they are not ashamed of expressing their feelings. The men have a far harder time. They are offered on-the-spot counseling to help deal with particularly traumatic situations. How I wish we had this. Every now and then someone at work says to me, "You should get danger pay." I would settle for counseling, or "debriefing."

While waiting for a carwash, not too long after witnessing the horror of the immediate aftermath of a drive-by shooting, I noticed a cop in the adjacent chair reading the Bible. I interrupted him to ask how he handles his work.

"As you see," he said. "I turn to the Good Book to remind myself that there is some reason for our being here, doing what we do. I also value the times people are pleased to see us, because there are those times as well."

Many of my coworkers, as well as the patients, are deeply religious. In their homes I see well-worn leather-bound copies of the Old and New Testament, open on coffee tables or bedside tables, with words highlighted or underscored. People can and do quote verses and chapters from the Bible.

I have been directed to the Book of Revelations, the Book of Daniel, and The Prophets. I ordered a hospital bed for a patient with bone cancer who was failing rapidly. One morning, shortly after he received his equipment, his sister called requesting that

I take the bed back, as he had been hospitalized. I asked whether he would be coming home. Her answer was to refer me to Revelations, chapter 22, and some chapters in Jeremiah. A simple yes or no answer on her part would have sufficed, but I dutifully went home and read those chapters. I still didn't know whether he would or would not be returning home. What I read frightened the hell out of me, however. That is, I think, what it's supposed to do.

From the time I first immigrated to Israel, I promised myself I would read the Bible, but I never did. I envy people their faith; they have something to turn to in a world gone mad. Also, they appear more accepting of whatever conditions prevail in their homes, their lives, on the streets, in the country, and in the world. I would love to take solace in religion, or in truly believing in a force greater than us. I want to believe that things happen for a reason, and that life is not just random and merciless. At certain times in my life I have believed in a unifying force, something which guides our actions, but my belief has cracks and fissures; it is far from being as steady and all-encompassing as the faith of so many of those with whom I work.

A 350-pound woman of fifty years who had spent the past year in a chair, unable to stand because of her weight and crippling rheumatoid arthritis, lived in an area where shootings and violence were an everyday occurrence. She did not flinch at the sound of gunshots or sirens. "If you read the Bible," she said to me, "it's all there, everything that is happening, it is all there." These are the same words I hear repeated by so many patients, no matter what class or race.

One day, as I gathered my files to leave the office for my visits, I was somewhat startled when a new clerk, a recent arrival from Texas, said to me, "Lord, girl, I pray for you, you're going to die and go to hell." Alarmed, I worried that she might know something I did not know about my upcoming day.

"I will die for sure," I informed her, "sooner or later, but I don't worry about hell. As far as I'm concerned, we're already experiencing it."

"No, no," she said. "If you accept the Lord in your heart, you won't go to hell."

In a hurry to leave, I replied that I am not a particularly bad person.

"Don't matter, you will go to hell if you don't accept the Lord into your heart."

Sighing, I left the office, unconvinced and unconverted.

Chapter 36

In 1997 the BBA (Balanced Budget Act) passed, with some provisions effective immediately, and some to be implemented gradually, until 2004. One of the changes was new annual caps on Medicare payments to home-care companies, in order to limit out-of-control and potentially fraudulent use of the benefit. For us this meant that, because of the decrease in Medicare reimbursement, the county cost in the agency would increase, and this could not be sustained. After closing one of the offices and removing public health nurses, the logical next step was to "curb" services to patients.

The home health agency also had to cut more positions, creating an increased workload for those lucky enough to still be there. Nurses had to maintain a productivity standard of 5 visits a day, and therapists 4.5. "Excess" staff time for home health aides and PT and OT staff was to be offered to other programs within the county. The salaries and benefits of these staff would be paid by the other programs and subtracted from the home health agency budget.

No mention was made of our patients, most of whom were very ill, which is why they needed our services in the first place. They were so debilitated, and befuddled by the drugs they were taking, that it took them quite some time to process instructions, or to try out new and unfamiliar equipment. How could we expect them to remember or carry out any new procedures barked at them by workers in a desperate hurry to get on to the next "consumer"?

A doctor referred a patient, a man in his late thirties with a dreadful hereditary disease that caused degeneration of the cerebellum. The disease made him appear to either be drunk or on drugs, as he could not maintain his balance and his speech was slurred. Because of this, and the disease process itself, he could be belligerent. Also, he wanted to maintain his independence and refused to admit that it was increasingly difficult for him to live alone. His mother, who had already lost her husband and another son to this disease, came by daily to help him bathe and prepare his meals. He did not take kindly to her help, either, sometimes not letting her in, sometimes shouting and cursing at her. The doctor warned us to be patient, nonthreatening, and gentle with the man.

At the end of the day, after his first visit, Big Bill sat at his desk and turned to face me, his snake earring flashing in the late afternoon sun. The man had said something to him that he could not understand. He had to ask him to repeat himself a few times. Eventually the man managed to blurt out, a little more clearly, "I said 'Fuck off,'" and with that he shoved Big Bill toward the door. Now I had to go and, because of the new regulations, would have to do my evaluation as quickly as possible.

I waited twenty minutes for him to reach his door. The stench of urine and feces hit me like a blow from a shovel when he finally opened it. To add to all his indignities, he was incontinent of both bladder and bowels. I was shocked to note that he crawled back to the bedroom on his hands and knees, and even so he bumped against the walls. And he had been a physical education teacher! His speech was slurry and thick, as if his tongue were pushing against a wall of molasses. It took me a few minutes to understand "Come in." I could not race through this evaluation. Mentally I calculated how to juggle my time so that I could listen to him and consult on what he needed. Would I manage to see 4.5 people today? What was the damn .5 supposed to be, anyway? Yet another day without time for lunch. Sitting down to eat was a rare occurrence, even though a nutritionist in Mill Valley had told me that in order to maintain my health and lower my stress level I must eat a leisurely, nutritious lunch in a beautiful setting. Poor man was deluded.

On another occasion I waited outside the door of a gunshot victim for at least half an hour. He was alone in the house.

Because he was paralyzed from his waist down, I knew he had to haul himself to a sitting position in his bed, using the trapeze bar. He then had to use a sliding board to get into his wheelchair, which, hopefully, had been placed next to his bed. After that he had to negotiate his way through narrow doorways and passages to get to the door and open it. The physical therapist assigned to his case had apparently not waited, because she was so concerned about completing her quota for the day. When he reached the door he was sweating, panting, and still furious that she had left. I had to bear the brunt of his anger that day. Inwardly I was mad at her, the county, and the whole goddamn system. Outside I remained cool and made excuses for her disappearance.

Another time I called a woman I had been trying unsuccessfully to contact. At last, one morning, I was pleased to hear a live voice on the phone. She said it was okay to come by, but soon, because she had a doctor's visit later that morning. Yes, I could, I was gathering my clipboard and papers and was on my way.

One look at me when I entered her small and cluttered apartment, reams of paper in my hands, rendered her tearful. She suffered from multiple sclerosis, which had affected the musculature in her arms and hands. It took her a long time to bathe and dress. Her mind was clouded by medication, slowing her responses even more. Now here I was, as she struggled to get herself and her daughter ready, filling in form after form after form, and asking inane questions like "Do you have access to running water?"

"Is there electricity?"

"Does individual reside with others?"

"What is the primary language in the home?"

I filled in the answers while she slowly braided her daughter's hair. The woman wanted to get ready without me scrutinizing her every move, and I totally understood, but I had to complete my evaluation, noting activities she could not perform independently. Whenever I saw she was experiencing difficulty, for instance, in raising her arms to shoulder level to braid her daughter's hair, I pounced upon her, giving her exercises and instructions to improve her performance. I had to do this so that I could honestly enter this in the area of the forms reserved for "skilled intervention." If I just filled in forms and did not provide instructions, the cost of my visit would not be covered.

She was also required to sign and date confidentiality forms, right-to-privacy forms, verification of visit, and insurance forms. If she was okay before I began, halfway through my visit she was exhausted.

It was impossible to complete our paperwork, the equivalent of a telephone directory, during visits. I stayed up long after most sane people had gone to bed, trying to remember what I had seen and done and write it within the required twenty-four hours: I had twenty-four hours after my initial visit to hand this in, in order to obtain approval for more visits, or equipment, or for these to be refused.

We all became increasingly frustrated and short-tempered, especially when we heard the nursing supervisor relentlessly grilling doctors and charge nurses who called to refer patients. "What do you mean, the patient needs her dressing changed daily? Can't her husband do it?" Never mind that the husband is eighty years old, does not have all his wits about him, and is riddled with arthritis. Many times she rudely refused to accept the consumer and then had the nerve to tell us referrals were low. Of course they were, no one in their right mind wanted to be questioned as to the wisdom of a referral.

She and my supervisor spoke behind closed doors for hours upon hours. What on earth did they talk about? They also spent days in Martinez, the county seat, in meetings. The amount of time administrators spent in meetings could definitely have been used far more productively, like in direct patient care.

If anyone dared interrupt me while I sat at my desk scribbling away, I tended to sigh and utter something gruff. We were all losing it. I heard a previously patient and mild-mannered nurse shout into the mouthpiece of her phone, "Win, W-I-N, my name is pronounced *Win*. N-G-U-Y-E-N, *Win!*"

Whenever I paused for a moment to look up from my paperwork, I saw nurses, aides, and other workers flying through the entrance, brows furrowed, sighing, lugging equipment whilst balancing piles of paperwork. Any case conferencing was carried out by shouting to each other while running past a desk or out the door. The final effect was like that of children playing broken telephone. No one finished conversations. The clerks had long ago quit their bantering and resembled the photos of America's Most Wanted. Hollow-eyed, they hunched over keyboards and monitors, ignoring ergonomic concerns as they struggled to enter our copious, squiggly notes into databases.

. . .

The layoffs and cutbacks continued. Suddenly registered nurses were no longer there. We were told they had moved on to different positions, one to the hospital, one to work with the homeless. At least they were still with the county.

It became increasingly difficult to find a healthy balance in my life. I went to the gym, hiked around the marina, looked at sunsets. I took up belly dancing and practiced meditation, trying to still my mind. One night, in desperation, I discovered a couple of TV shows, *Cops* and *Rescue 911*. So much for my previous stress relievers, these shows were great. It helped to know that someone else was having a worse time than me. And while I drove, did I listen to the classical music station? To jazz? To NPR or KPFA? No, I listened to Garth Brooks, LeAnn Rimes, Lyle Lovett, Reba McEntire, and desperately searched for the always disappearing country music stations.

So much of what I saw haunted me. Patients appeared in my dreams, floating on ceilings, wheelchairs suspended in air. Sometimes, try as I might, I could not leave the images I saw behind at the office. My gorge rose as I drove home, trying to get rid of the stench I carried from a bilateral amputee whose stumps had turned gangrenous. I thought about the paperwork I still had to complete, the equipment I needed to order.

CHAPTER 37

It had been a long day. The temperature was in the sizzling 100s. I couldn't put on my seatbelt without first covering the steel clasp with a cloth. I spread a towel across my car seat so that I could sit without incurring second degree burns on the backs of my thighs.

I was on my way to a new referral, an elderly woman by the name of Josephine who lived in a board and care facility. I knocked on the front door of a neat, white home set in a shady garden. An old lady with the ruddy, broken-capillaried skin and watery eyes of a seasoned drinker opened it.

Before I could say anything she beseeched me, "Take me away, take me away." I had been prepared to ask this woman where I could find Josephine, but after hearing her words and looking into her eyes, I realized she might not be the one in charge of this establishment.

A Filipino woman frying egg rolls in the kitchen turned around to observe this scene. Without a word she turned her back on us and continued frying.

I asked her for Josephine.

Flipping the egg rolls, she said, "Look for Josephine yourself, ma'am."

A woman tottering around unsteadily in the back garden answered to the name of Josephine. Her purple jumpsuit bore specks of food, and a thick, creamy substance coated her tongue and oozed out of the corners of her mouth. It dripped down onto her jumpsuit, forming a sticky base for the crumbs that had fallen there previously, maybe from breakfast? Dinner the night before? Lunch before then? Trying to mask my revulsion,

I explained who I was and asked whether we could go to her room.

"Vy, ja, surely," she replied in a thick German accent, although from the way she looked at me and the long time she took to respond, I realized she had no clue of who I might be or what I wanted. Being polite was probably deeply ingrained. Following her slowly as she teetered back toward the house, I entered the living room, where three old women sat on a sofa staring at *General Hospital*. One lady's tongue lolled out of the side of her mouth, writhing in undulating spasms. Three pairs of eyes followed us as Josephine wandered from room to room, peering inside, then shaking her head. Obviously she could not remember her room. I noticed her name on a door, painted neatly on white tile bordered by pink roses, and asked whether that was her room.

She looked inside. "Oh, ja, let's go in and sit."

She plopped down on the bed, which was made up neatly and covered with a pink and beige floral bedcover. She gestured for me to sit on a nearby chair upholstered in the same material. I sat down, clipboard on my lap, wondering why the nurse had asked me to come. As was all too often the case, not much was written on the referral. Maybe I had been sent to ensure Josephine's safety? She did not walk very steadily. For the sake of privacy I closed the door and began asking her questions. While I wrote I heard someone close by say, in an unaccented voice, "Stephanie, you shit, get me water. Pete, where are you? Leave me alone, goddamn it."

A deep male voice said, "Drink your water, bitch."

Startled, I looked around the room. No one else was there. I stared at Josephine, who looked at me and smiled, waiting for my next question.

"Do you hear voices?" I asked.

"No," she said, "no voices. There are other people in the room, and I need to talk to them."

"Okay," I said, hastily gathering my papers and clipboard. "I'll leave you then, thanks for your time."

Shaking my head in disbelief, I drove back to the office in the blistering heat, wondering, for the umpteenth time, what I was doing, and why, and whether I should apply for a position at Nordstrom.

CHAPTER 38

Many times over the years, I would sit at my desk before setting out for the day, surveying my caseload while sipping my latte. A man in his thirties who had fractured both legs jumping over a high wall at 2:00 a.m. For once I decided to quell my curiosity and not ask whom or what he was running from. A man of twenty-three from North Richmond who had survived his second shooting this year. As his condition improved with each successive visit, his demeanor changed. The first time, I saw a scared little boy in pain. Now, as his strength and mobility returned, he was preparing to go back to the streets. His language contained more and more "mans"—"Man, you know, man, that's how it is, man. I want the person who shot me to feel my pain, man." Each time I visited his clothes were sharper; expensive sneakers, baggy striped pants. On my last visit a heavy gold chain hung around his neck.

Why am I doing this? My constant refrain. And, as usual, at that moment I could not come up with any good reason. Right then my greatest pleasure was the morning latte I bought from a drive-through espresso hut. (Starbucks had not yet taken over the planet.) Surely this access to lattes was as good a reason as any for continuing this work. The reality is that deep down inside I still harbored the conviction that we were effecting a positive change, or at least that my being there and listening to someone could be of some help.

Many times I thought I was losing my grip on sanity, and I wondered if this was stress-induced, or if the people I saw were truly as crazy as I seemed to find them. After such visits I needed to return to the office and consult with my colleagues for a reality check. Of course, in our increasingly crazed states, this was not always of value.

This referral was to a woman with nothing worse than lower extremity cellulitis, hypertension, and venous stasis ulcers. After a month of dealing with extremely involved patients and families, this seemed a breeze, even though the referral also stated that her husband had Alzheimer's. When I called the patient she was welcoming, but I did experience a twinge of doubt when she gave me directions. I was familiar with the exits near her home and asked which one to take. She was unable to recall the names of any of them.

Nevertheless, I reached her home without difficulty. A large crack in a glass pane of the front door was covered with brown paper and duct tape. The wind blew hard, causing the glass to vibrate alarmingly. Cloth was stuffed into the hole where the door handle should be. This was not out of the ordinary. A tall, unshaven, gray-haired man answered the door. He invited me in and pulled up a chair. He sat down between me and his wife, who was sitting on a low chair. At first glance I noticed a tremor in her right hand and arm, even when she was at rest. When I asked her to sign her name on the forms, she said she could not, as her thumb wasn't working. She asked whether her husband could sign for her. He took the paper and asked me where to sign. I pointed to the large red stamp that read "verification of visit" (one of the new requirements) with a line for the signature.

"What should I write, and where?" he queried.

"Your signature, on the red line above 'verification of visit.'"

"My name?"

"Yes, you can use your name."

"Her name?"

"No, yours," I repeated, my heart sinking.

"Shouldn't I sign her name?"

"Go on," said his wife, "Sign your name like the lady said."

Then she turned to me.

"I don't know what you or anyone wants. I'm fine. These people irritate me. We just got rid of some people who came about a lawsuit I have with a car dealer. Here, look at this letter from the Department of Motor Vehicles."

"Actually, I don't need to see it," I said. "That's not why I am here. I need to ask you some questions."

When I asked her how she bathed, she looked at me straight in the eyes for the first time since my arrival and said, "I don't bathe, I'm allergic to water."

"Water?"

"Yes." She turned her head to the side again. "These people, they all ask me why water?"

With that she let out a long, loud belch.

"That's the pectin in the capsules I take, I'm allergic to pectin. In the book of Paul it is written that ye must fast and drink wine. I can't drink wine because of the alcoholism in my family, my brother is an alcoholic. It makes me mad that you ask about bathing, I hate being asked that. I'm sorry for getting mad, but here, this is what I drink."

She pushed a paper cup containing a light red liquid toward me.

"Taste it, go on." she pushed the cup into my hand.

I sniffed the mixture, which smelled tart, and put the cup down.

"No, drink it."

Could this be an electric Kool-Aid acid test, or is she a female Jim Jones? I wondered. I pretended to sip, swallowing loudly, then put the cup down again.

"That is what I drink, as it is commanded," she said, pointing to a Bible on a stool close by. "Grain vinegar. I can't touch apple cider vinegar because I am allergic to apples. Grain vinegar with two packets of NutraSweet and I add Kool-Aid. I worked it out myself, this cleanses me. See this rash under my breast? She raised her right arm, which was no longer trembling, unbuttoned her blouse with her left hand, pushed aside a pendulous breast, and pointed to a red rash. "I put lard on that, it's fine."

161

Her husband looked from me to her, riveted, like watching a tennis match at Wimbledon.

"He lost his memory—not really, he remembers things. They said he has early Alzheimer's, but I cured that, I got rid of my fridge."

Abruptly she ended this monologue. Her husband's head stopped midway, as if the tennis ball had frozen in midair. The words "I got rid of my fridge" hung in the air between us.

Stupefied, I sat there, not knowing what to say. I thought she looked relatively clean for someone who had stopped bathing years go. I noted that the living room was bare but saw piles of clothing lying on top of a bed in another room. I looked at my watch and wondered what I would tell the doctor about this meeting. "The lady is nuts, out of her mind, completely bonkers" seemed the best, most professional thing to say.

"See, we manage fine. It was the carbon dioxide and we got rid of it." Her voice interrupted my thoughts.

Piecing the patches of sentences together, I realized she thought her husband's now nonexistent Alzheimer's had been caused by carbon dioxide emitted from the large fridge. At least I supposed that is what she thought, but I had no desire to ask her if this were indeed so.

I managed an elegant exit, all the while cursing the nurse who had sent me. The nurses were often on the receiving end of my silent curses, and I hoped the unkind thoughts I sent in their direction would not actually work. Wasn't I supposed to be practicing positive thinking and compassion?

. . .

I wish I could say the Kool-Aid lady was the last patient of the day, but she wasn't. I had my quota of patients to fill. The next was a single man who lived with the family of a former business acquaintance in Pacheco. Apparently no one had a clear idea of what was ailing this man. He had been belligerent to the doctors, the nurses, and the physical therapist. Now it was my turn to figure out what was ailing his body, mind, or both.

His room was on the second floor, on the left side of a dark, unlit staircase in a dark, rambling home. A gruff-looking woman with red cheeks and short salt-and-pepper hair let me in. She pointed down a dark passageway to the stairwell. The words of a Texan woman I had treated came back to me: "It's as dark as a stack of black cats in here." I stumbled along, feeling my way with my hands, hoping I wouldn't trip and break something. This was definitely not a safe environment. I would have to suggest many changes, and I was not too sure how my suggestions would be received, judging by the nasty and harassed demeanor of the woman who had opened the door.

Lying in bed was a man about forty years old. He had a shock of dark brown hair. I had barely entered the room when he proceeded to tell me, in a whiny, nasal voice, how everything hurt. He couldn't move any part of his body, not even his toes or his fingers, without pains that crept up and down his arms and legs. He couldn't get out of bed. In fact, he couldn't turn over in bed. He had, surprise, been a truck driver when these strange sensations overcame him. They began in his toes and moved up his calves. The people he was staying with were helping him. He and the man had been partners prior to his becoming ill, but he could not rely on their charity forever. He had applied for Medi-Cal, but it hadn't come through. He didn't like the county doctors—they didn't believe him, no one could find anything wrong, but he was not crazy, everything hurt. It all hurt so much that even wearing clothing was agonizing. That probably explained his outfit: yellow stained underpants. He howled like a banshee when I lightly brushed his shoulder. While he whined on and on and on, I noticed that he came to a sitting position on the side of the bed. He had said he couldn't sit or move any parts of his body. Did he levitate? I hadn't noticed that. Did he think I was blind, or really stupid? I mean, what went on in his mind, if he had one?

As he rambled on, he moved his legs and gesticulated with his arms. Did he not think I would notice these discrepancies? I pointed out that I had seen him move. This observation caused him to shout at me. He had thought I understood him. We were all the same. No one believed him. He was in pain, he could not move, he was sick, very sick, probably dying.

He was also well aware of the equipment and help he could receive when he did receive Medi-Cal. He wanted a special bed with a mattress to prevent pressure spots. He wanted a commode, but I reminded him that he couldn't move, so he would not be able to use one. Without even pausing for a second, he asked for an aide who could help him onto the commode and sponge bathe him. Moreover, he needed someone to prepare meals. I grew speechless. He even had the audacity to ask for a TV, because no one could expect him to just lie in bed doing nothing all day long. Reading was out of the question, because how could he hold a book? This man was not open to helpful suggestions.

I drove home feeling numb, reading bumper stickers that changed with the political climate of the neighborhood. "Don't Steal, the Government Hates Competition." "Keep Abortion Legal." I saw a red truck flying past and caught a glimpse of a long-haired driver with a peaked cap turned backward. His bumper sticker proclaimed, "Redneck."

. . .

At the office the next morning, I told the per diem physical therapist about the Kool-Aid lady. She looked at me with her expressionless face, then asked whether I had gone to see the strange man afterward. She'd had a similar experience with him and was as baffled as everyone else. As I described my visit, I noticed that the flesh on the outer corners of her eyes crinkled, the corners of her mouth turned up, and a strange new sound came out of her mouth. To my utter amazement, she was laughing. I began to laugh as well. The two of us howled, leaning over, arms clasped around our waists, until tears rolled down our cheeks. After I had calmed down sufficiently, I called the doctor who had referred the man. He listened to my description of the visit in silence punctuated by heavy breathing. Then I heard something like a sigh breaking his silence. He confessed that by the time he and the attending psychologist had finished interviewing the man, they both felt like hitting him with a baseball bat to put him out of his misery, then hanging themselves. Such was this man's effect upon people. No one knew what was going on with him. There were no clinical signs of any specific disease, but his whiny and decidedly odd affect was having rippling effects. Sadly, maybe he was ill, but no one believed him.

We did send an aide, a large gentle woman with a soothing voice and comforting hands. After her first visit, he only wanted her to care for him, declining nurses and therapists. He even offered to hire her privately, although previously he had stated that he was as poor as a church mouse. She declined his offer because, she said, as tempting as the extra money was, she would end up crazy if she went there daily.

This man definitely knew how to "manipulate the system," as the nursing supervisor was so fond of saying. He received a hospital bed, a commode (never used), and a wheelchair. He could not get downstairs to the wheelchair and refused to sit in it anyway, saying it was too uncomfortable. When we could no longer justify visits from the aide he "fired" us, to our collective delight, and apparently asked for another home health agency. We later heard from them that he had fired them as well.

CHAPTER 39

On a daily basis, I declared that nothing, neither the situations, the people, nor the homes we entered, could surprise me anymore. Every day I was surprised and shocked anew by the situations and the squalor. I entered homes full to the brim with newspapers dating back to when the inhabitants were born, piled high on every available surface, blocking access to passageways and rooms. Mouse droppings on kitchen counters provided an obstacle course for armies of ants. The plumbing did not work, toilets were backed up. Every room of a house I went to was full of birds: finches, budgerigars, parrots, cockatiels, and more, either in cages or flying around, alighting on the kitchen table and nightstands. Cages of finches were in the shower and bathroom as well, leaving the bird-loving residents nowhere to bathe. I sneezed, coughed, and spluttered, apparently allergic to at least one of the many species of birds in this home. Moreover, I was alarmed by the fluttering of wings, as well as by large boa constrictors curled up in warm pockets of living rooms. Neither did I think tarantulas made for loving little pets.

There were the uber-done. A woman showed up at her front door in flannel pajamas bearing a decoration of cows jumping over moons. She looked like she had been cute before being ravaged by liver cancer. She was petite, with a Texas-size head of blond hair which, she soon confessed, was a wig—quickly adding that her hair had been just the same. Her entire neat apartment was decorated with cows: cow curtains, cow bedspreads, cow pillows, cow kettles, cow milk pitchers, cow salt-and-pepper sets. I thought she had been raised on a dairy or cattle farm, but no, she was born and raised in Concord and had worked as a waitress in a diner all her life, until illness struck her down.

In contrast to the uber-done, there were those who did not think clothing necessary, even in the presence of an unknown health-care worker. From the front door of a home, a loud female voice bellowed at me to come in. I walked in to find an enormous woman sitting on the bed stark naked. Rolls of flesh cascaded downward. The side of her head that first presented itself was a mass of tight black snarls fanning out like a thundercloud. She turned to face me. The other side was parted in long cornrows. Hair extensions spread out over a chair near the bed. The woman standing next to her braiding her hair reached for the strands, then wove them into her hair. A paper plate with a half-eaten hamburger and fries lay on the bed, near the extensions. The supposedly ill patient smoked and joked with the braider, occasionally turning to acknowledge my presence by telling me she needed a wheelchair, she needed a commode, she needed a walker. What she needed was to put on some clothing, stop smoking, stop eating junk, get up, and move.

Not everyone was stark raving mad or lived in shabby, unkempt homes or animal-themed environments. That would have made my work impossible. Many homes were havens. I felt privileged to meet warm and wonderful human beings without guile or pretense.

I was asked to evaluate an elderly woman, Mrs. Angie, who had recently become weak and fallen while bathing. We sat on either side of her coffee table. A framed picture of Martin Luther King Jr. decorated a wall, alongside pictures of large-eyed babies, smiling children, teenagers, and a young man in military uniform. Books lined the shelves of the salon, including Alex Haley's *Roots* and what appeared to be a multi-volume encyclopedia of black history. Recent copies of *Essence* and *Ebony* magazines covered the coffee table. A large, worn, leather-bound Bible, opened to the Book of Jeremiah, lay next to a black Barbie doll's head, which emerged proudly from a red and white dress, hand-crocheted in the style of a flamenco dancer's flouncy skirts. Hand-sewn dolls, stuffed animals, hand-crocheted afghans, and embroidered items were carefully placed on tables, dressers, and beds. I admired these objects and told her I used to knit and crochet back when I had time, so I appreciated the work and care that went into these items.

"Until recently I attended the Richmond Senior Center," said Mrs. Angie. "Seems like I don't have too much energy to go there these days, but it sure was fun. We made a whole lot of things. Come, I'll show you." She took me into her room and pulled a quilt out of the tidy closet. Together we unfolded it. The quilt felt heavy and was bigger than a king-size bed. In the middle a large yellow star burst from a pulsating center into many points. The star was evenly stitched onto blue cloth the color of cornflowers. The quilt was bordered in red. The effect was spectacular.

"My last job before retiring was in Walnut Creek, caring for a little white boy," Mrs. Angie told me. "Lord, I loved that child and his family. I had been with them for a few years when he attended his first day of school. I anxiously waited for him to come home so I could hear about his day. When he returned he looked at me and the first thing he said was, 'Mrs. Angie, why are you black?'

"Holding his hand, I took him to their garden. 'Look,' I said, 'What do you see?'

"'Flowers.'

"'Are they all the same? Do they have the same colors and smells?'

"'No.'

"'And they're all beautiful. Just like the Lord made different flowers, he made different people, too.' He understood what I was saying."

So did I. Most of us don't compare the beauty of flowers.

"I grew up in Arizona. We was all the same. We'd all swim in a creek, white kids, Mexicans, Indians. But then the Mormons complained about us dark ones, and we had to go swim else-where, but that was okay. It didn't bother us, we just upped and found us another waterhole.

"Back then everything was natural, you know, the food and stuff. We didn't want for anything. We grew our vegetables. My job was to churn the butter. Everything tasted so good, real fresh, not like now. Seems like I don't have no appetite no more." She looked into the kitchen and smiled a little, then her smile disappeared and she looked somewhat sad. "No, things just aren't the same."

Eventually Mrs. Angie just faded quietly, and with dignity, into the long night which awaits us all.

. . .

A woman of eighty-one years whose face resembled that of the Madonna (not the singer) in its unlined calm and serenity lived with her daughter and grandchildren. She had had so many joints replaced secondary to debilitating degenerative joint disease that she referred to herself as a bionic woman. She was recuperating from a second hip replacement, and that was how I met her. Stepping into the house, situated in a neighborhood on the verge of becoming seedy, felt like entering a Norman Rockwell haven. The warm, comforting aroma of freshly baked, buttery cinnamon cookies filled the cocoon. Her daughter lay on the couch across from her mom, her young son asleep in her arms. A two-year-old boy on a recliner dozed in his grandfather's arms. I wanted to remain there forever, doing nothing but breathing in the cinnamon aroma and listening to the deep and calm voices of the women.

The matriarch told me that none of her large brood of grandkids had ever been in trouble. "Kids need to know they have someone to come home to after school. We all love each other, and we all go to church every Sunday."

And indeed, it was impossible not to be affected by the aura of love that filled the home. It penetrated me as well, and accompanied me for the rest of the day, tinting my day in an amber, honey-colored glow.

Simple lives, simple truths.

CHAPTER 40

The diagnoses on the referrals we receive are brief, written in a hurry by the nurse or physical therapist making the referral. Male or female born in x year, followed by a string of acronyms: MS (multiple sclerosis), SCI (spinal cord injury), CVA (cerebral vascular accident), TBI (traumatic brain injury), GSW (gunshot wound), MVA (motor vehicle accident), TIA (transient ischemic attack), and so on. Many conditions I had never heard of, and could happily have lived the rest of my life without knowing about. It is disturbing to become intimately acquainted with the infinite number of ways one can become ill, or die; to know the horror that can befall one from outside sources, like a fall from a ladder while changing a light bulb, or from diseases that creep up silently, attacking from one's core. Yet another reminder to live in, and be grateful for, each moment of health, clarity, vitality.

No matter how brief or terse the referral, I remind myself that this person is an individual, a family member, a parent, a neighbor, a friend. Everyone has a story, no one is just a string of illnesses. I do my best to listen to them and to put myself in their place so that I can better understand what they must be feeling, and what they truly need. So many just need someone to listen to them.

Occasionally I entered a home feeling fine and left feeling sad and weighed down, only to hear the person say, "Well thanks, I feel really good now." Of course they were better, I had taken on their burdens. Because of this trait of mine, I have had to learn to protect myself, and it has been an important lesson for me. When I worked as a therapist in Israel I did not know how to do this and soon became burnt-out. Time and experience have helped me.

Every day offers opportunities and challenges. The way in which I deal with these can leave me cynical, exhausted, burnt-out, or exhilarated, filled with joy and gratitude. I experience all these emotions numerous times during the course of a day. I am forced to face my own prejudices and limits, the things I want, and those that are no longer of any importance. Always, when I return home I give thanks for the fact that I am safe, that I have a roof over my head (albeit a rented one), that I have food to eat, good health, and friends. I never take anything for granted—or, I should say, I try not to.

I began to understand what is meant by "as the macrocosm, so the microcosm." Despite our outward differences—religion, culture, food, customs—we are all basically the same. Everyone is trying to survive. Everyone needs food and desires health and a good or "better" life for their children than they had. Births, marriages, graduations, rites of passage are celebrated every-where. We share the same joys, worries, and tragedies. Suffer-ing, also, is the same, whether in inner cities or in secluded, lux-urious homes. Granted, it is more private in luxurious homes, and the inhabitants do not have the added burden of constant, erosive worry about money and how to pay for everything, from basic necessities like food and rent to medications. Our differences are defined by the manner in which we prioritize our choices, by the amount of money we have, by our belief systems and practices, by prevailing political situations, by how we perceive our places in the universe, and by how we exist with the only constant: change.

Because of the ever shifting rules of work, I had to adapt to change as often as a new wave breaks onshore. This made me realize how easy it is in theory to say one must live with this constant, and how very difficult it is in fact. I found myself wish-ing for change to slow its relentless pace, and when I was left breathless I was really grateful for my garden and the lessons from the earth.

Standing next to my gigantic rosemary bush, which had grown from a small branch I placed in the yard, I remembered how living on the kibbutz had its own special rhythm. Time itself had a texture to it, a gentle pull and tug as it wove between the softly curving landscape of the Western Galilee, each season transforming the hills around us. The short, breathtaking spring, with its white almond blossoms, pink blossoms, wild poppies, expanses of lupine, cyclamen, violets, and carpets of wildflowers that turned into green fields, themselves becoming platinum, gold, and copper. And then everything was scorched from the sun, brown, dusty, all waiting for the first rains. Then time returned, to wind its spiral way yet again. Change was evident, but it did not leave us gasping at its swift pace, wondering where time had gone.

If I learned anything from this work, it was to suspend judgment. So many of those I saw did not live or function according to societal norms, but they were survivors, people who were born into horrendous circumstances, often with little or no education. To survive, they did what they knew best, living by their wits. Contrary to the New Age belief system, I do not believe they chose these conditions. How nice if it were that simple: if, through magical thinking, one could change one's reality, manifest prosperity and health, and live happily ever after. Although often I was witness to terrible alienation, I also experienced love and caring so palpable that its presence filled homes like a golden cloud, softly enveloping those within. A large man, so muscle-bound and daunting he probably causes people to check whether their car doors are locked, gently lifts his cancer-ridden brother from the hospital bed. Tenderly he bathes and massages him, pats him dry, and smoothes lotion onto his emaciated frame, then carefully places him in his wheelchair. I come across families who refuse to place parents in homes. "This is my mom, she raised me, now it is my turn," says a tough-looking young man as he spoon-feeds his mother, strokes her hair, wipes away her drool, and changes her diapers.

I feel caring from the community as well.

Tree Barking

"How do you get into your tub?" I asked a man who had a stroke. He had a claw-foot tub that was very difficult to climb in and out of.

"My neighbor from across the street comes over to pick me up. He's a retired football player."

Neighbors come by unannounced. "Hey, I'm going shopping, you need something?"

"Sure, I can fix a ramp for you, no problem."

CHAPTER 41

I evaluated an old woman who had undergone a quadruple bypass and was unable to safely climb over the small step into her shower. She could not bathe herself without having to sit down, gasping for breath. The surgery scars that flared an angry deep purple down the front of her chest impeded her ability to use her arms to bathe, brush her teeth, comb her hair, and dress. She lived alone. This was after we had been told to cut visits down to a bare minimum, the initial evaluation and one to follow up. I requested Medicare to authorize two more visits after my initial evaluation. My request was denied as not being necessary. Under the latest guidelines, teaching this woman how to manage these activities through exercise and energy conservation would not be reimbursed.

An article appeared in an occupational therapy magazine, stating, in euphemistic terms, that "OTs are being presented with new challenges and opportunities as the provisions of the Balanced Budget Act (BBA) of 1997 are implemented." New challenges and opportunities, how exciting. "Administrators and practitioners in home health care have been inundated by new rules for reporting and payment, with some being implemented retroactively or only days after being announced." In other words, many of the visits we made would not be covered. The county was losing money; we would lose our jobs; the patients would not receive care.

In addition, we received notices and letters full of acronyms, "The HCFA [Health Care Financing Administration] released a notice in the Federal Register alerting HHAs [home health agencies] of the effective dates for OASIS [Outcomes and Assessment Information Set] implementation." OASIS provides the HCFA with a way to monitor the effectiveness of the services that Medicare pays for. For thirty years, Medicare payments had been related not to how effective a service was or how efficiently it was provided, but to whether the provider had followed all of Medicare's standards and regulations. Because payment was made per visit on the basis of what it cost the home health agency to provide the treatment, inefficiency (accomplishing less in more visits) was rewarded with more revenue.

I remember the unnecessary number of visits my supervisor told us to request when I first began: we were being reimbursed for them, so the more visits, the better.

"The purpose of the OASIS," a questionnaire we now had to take with us that contained seventy-eight questions in addition to our evaluation, "is to provide the HCFA with a way to examine the performance of a home health care agency relative to other agencies in the same geographic region or nationwide. It also allows HCFA to give feedback to a provider regarding its performance compared with that of other providers so that the agency can implement appropriate performance improvement activities." In other words, cut down on patient service time, cut down on workers, streamline, and, like sharks, hone in for the kill, dealing with a patient just once, if possible.

What astounded me working in home health was seeing the waste incurred while the debate raged on about spiraling costs, and who should or should not receive care: seniors, children, the insured, the uninsured, and so on.

Many of those we saw live on fixed incomes, such as Social Security or welfare, which now fell under the new acronym of TANF (Temporary Assistance to Needy Families). These people cannot afford frills. Because many of the ill are bedridden, they develop pressure spots. Technically, these are called decubitus ulcers, or bedsores.

These sores are caused when parts of an ill, inert, or paralyzed body are in constant contact with a hard surface, such as a mattress. At first they look innocent, resembling blisters or red, shiny spots on the skin. However, these spots become like the proverbial tip of the iceberg. Underneath them, tunnels widen and invade the underlying fascia and connective tissue. Unless proper care is taken, they continue their destructive exploration downward to the bone, destroying everything in their path. The necrotic tissue has to be cut out, which usually requires lengthy hospitalization, and the surgery is not always successful. Prevention—ensuring they don't occur—is the optimal method of treatment for bedsores.

An egg-crate mattress costs under twenty dollars and can help prevent these sores. This may not seem like a lot of money, but it is to people on fixed incomes. Insurance does not cover this cost. They will, however, cover the enormous costs of hospitalization, surgery, skin grafts, et cetera.

In simulated home environments in rehabilitation centers and hospitals, paralyzed or otherwise disabled patients, like amputees or those with traumatic brain injury, are trained by physical and occupational therapists to make transfers from hospital beds to wheelchairs, bathtubs, showers, and toilets. They are sent home with the necessary equipment to make these transfers easier and safer. Most patients, however, cannot supply correct measurements of their entry doors, bathrooms, and kitchens, and no one goes to assess the environment before the patient is sent home. I see creative use being made of expensive and useless equipment. For example, a bath bench becomes a stand for potted plants or a TV. Laundry is draped over wheelchairs, and walkers become towel racks. Equipment can be and sometimes is put up for sale. For whatever reason, the equipment that was paid for by insurance cannot be returned, so more equipment is ordered.

Hospital beds are considered luxuries, only "justified' if the patient is about to die. Patients sleep on old and lumpy beds and mattresses: most of us don't buy beds with the idea that one day we may become bed-bound. These old beds make transfers difficult, even dangerous. And many patients who have always slept on the floor are not now, at the ends of their lives, about to get into a bed. It would save money to check patients' environment, culture, and personal requirements before sending equipment to their homes.

CHAPTER 42

My personal blow came January 14, 1999, when my supervisor approached me first thing in the morning, clicking her pen, and said she needed to speak to me urgently. Immediately after saying this, she vanished into the nursing supervisor's office, closed the door behind her, and sat down opposite the nurse. Since the cuts began, these two had spent hours behind closed doors, talking. What would I do? Apparently she had forgotten that she wanted to speak to me. While I made appointments to see patients (client consumers), I constantly looked in the direction of the closed door, waiting for her to emerge and return to her desk. I had to leave soon to make my quota. When, after an hour, she still had not emerged, I knocked on the door, poked my head in, and announced I had to leave—didn't she want to speak to me?

"Oh yes, come to my desk," she said, exiting the nursing supervisor's office. She kept her eyes downcast as she walked briskly to her desk.

She sat down and pushed aside the piles of papers that cluttered her desk, clearing her throat and clicking her ballpoint pen. She then pushed the piles to the other side and cleared her throat again. Why was she stalling? These actions infuriated me. Her right leg was crossed over her left leg and her right foot jiggled up and down, up and down. She looked at me directly for the first time, cleared her throat yet again, then said, "Look, this is nothing personal..." Just that phrase caused my heart to jump. "And it is no reflection on you, but as you know, you were the last therapist hired." Yes, I knew that, seven years ago. "The bean counters are looking at the numbers, and as you know (this seemed her favorite phrase), referrals have been very low. Nurses have been transferred to other departments or have taken a cut in pay to stay here. Now they are looking at the therapists. I can't say for sure when they will begin eliminating your positions, but I do know it will happen. You will be the first to go. I am telling you now so that you can make other plans." I was touched by her consideration. "You could stay with us on a per diem basis, but I know you need the benefits. It would be ideal if you could find a twenty-hour job with benefits outside the county, then work for us per diem. I will, of course, inquire as to whether there are other jobs within the county, but I doubt it. I'm going away for a week, and now you had better go and see the consumers. Bye."

I listened in shock, my heart racing. Suddenly I was overwhelmed by a feeling of numbness, unaware of any sensation except that I had begun shaking from the cold that no one else in the office seemed to be experiencing. A mist rose from my feet and swirled upward, encompassing my whole being, and I could not think clearly. Her terse words were uttered without any warmth or any emotion at all, in a clipped, cold tone, against the background of clicking and jiggling. I knew myself well enough to know that pretty soon my shock would be overtaken by anger. Then I would be able to think of many clever things to say. But right now, sitting at her desk, I remained uncharacteristically speechless.

That's it? Seven years of work ends like this? Boom, dash, without so much as a by-your-leave or thank-you. And now I am supposed to head out to see my client/consumers? I wondered how I should present myself. Smiling? Positive? Optimistic? My head reeled. Stunned, hurt, and shocked, I gathered my clipboard and papers and walked out of the office, trying to maintain a professional image and do the work I still cared so much about.

The first patient (I stubbornly refused to think of them as client/consumers) I was to see that day lived in a senior center in Richmond. When I called her to arrange a time, she wanted to know if I could bring her some food, "maybe something you have around the office."

As the recession worsened and conditions deteriorated, we encountered more and more people in dire situations with multiple needs. Because of the rising cost of medications, more patients had to choose between food, gas and electricity, and medications. Sometimes a patient's blood pressure rose mysteriously. After questioning we found out they had taken half a pill instead of the whole one, as prescribed, and only took it every other day because the medicine was so costly.

I informed her I could bring a bagel and cream cheese and I could get coffee on the way.

"No coffee, just a bagel will be lovely, honey."

Her tiny studio apartment was packed with stereo equipment and TVs, and I mean packed. Stacked against two walls were DVD players, VCRs, CD players, large TVs, small TVs. They were piled precariously, one on top of the other, almost reaching the ceiling. I had to squeeze in between this staggering display of high-tech equipment and a coffee table covered with potted plants. I made my short way to the sofa, then placed my clipboard next to the plants on the table. She sat next to me, a very attractive woman who was obviously not well. She had on a wig and her tight clothing showed her curvaceous figure to full advantage. At some point she claimed to be a distant cousin of Tina Turner, and judging by her looks, this may have been true. That she was not well was clear because of her ashen color and labored breathing. She was barely able to move from the sofa to the kitchen, maybe ten steps, without stopping to hold onto a TV or VCR, or a chair, for support. She stood there, her hand on a shelf, taking shallow, raspy breaths. She was on her way to the kitchen to put on the kettle to make tea to accompany our bagels. She apologized profusely for asking me to bring food and explained that her Social Security check had not yet arrived, and her monthly food allowance had run out.

Despite her weakened condition, she was a hoot. Slowly, because of her need to stop and suck in air, she told me that she had been a stripper in her earlier years. "Not that disgusting lap dancing," she told me. "I was a professional. I raised four children being a stripper. Now look at my place," she said, pointing to all the stereo equipment. "Do you think I need all this? Of course not. Remember that chemical leak at Chevron a few years back? That is why I am sick. They paid me money, but I can only use it on myself, not open up accounts for my children, so I bought all this stuff. Every now and then someone official calls to ask what I am doing with the money. They actually check with financial institutions to ensure I haven't opened up accounts. At least these things I can give my children, but there is a limit to what they need or want."

I found myself pouring my heart out to her. Not only was she very sympathetic, she was astute. She had been active in local politics, and people still called to ask her to speak at town meetings. She told me how heartbroken she was that her children did not share her political interests. "They grew up at a different time, honey. They don't know what we fought for. Now it is just guns and shooting. I vote because it is a privilege, and we must—otherwise we got no right to complain. The young people now just don't seem to care. In part I think it is because they are so disillusioned. No politician comes through with what they promise, but we just can't give up."

I told her I would return, whether or not I was allowed visits. We could eat together, work on energy conservation techniques, and she could try out a bath seat. Also, we would make her home a little safer, removing throw rugs and cords, and arranging her many potted plants so that they wouldn't fall, and she could have easy access to water them. But mainly, we could talk while, in the background, her amazing collection of jazz played.

That day I did not make my quota of patients. I just did not care. When I returned to the office my supervisor had left for the Martinez office, and the social worker was sitting in our cubbyhole. He had been there in the morning when my supervisor spoke to me and couldn't help but hear what she said, since we were not more than four feet away from him. That afternoon he turned around and asked how I was doing. This was different from his normal "Hey, how ya doin?" His eyes searched my face with concern. Then he said he had heard everything.

"Nesta, call your union. They are supposed to help their members. Tell them what she said. She can't just get rid of you."

Of these things I was unaware. I did know the union faithfully deducted dues from my salary every month, and I received reminders of meetings, but I had never met anyone from the union and so was totally unaware of what they did. I had never attended a union meeting. Actually, this was my first position in America that had a union, and I didn't understand their purpose. I did know that the clerks belonged to one union, social workers to another, nurses to another. My supervisor told us that the nurses' union was strong and fought for them, and that is why they earned such good salaries.

"According to union rules," the social worker said, swiveling around and around on his chair, "you cannot just be laid off, you have to be transferred to another position within the county, with the same hours, benefits, and salary. You can also keep your seniority." Swivel. "I heard what your supervisor said, and I know what is really going on." Swivel, swivel. "How and who can she supervise if you are all laid off? What she wants to do is get rid of you so she can work in your position in order to stay on with the county and get her benefits."

I listened to him in disbelief. This could not be true.

He continued. "In other words, she no longer wants to be in administration, because her position will be unnecessary." His next swivel and the accompanying words set my head spinning. "To save her butt she has to be a worker again, and she is an occupational therapist. This is her devious way of going about this. First she tells you that you have to go, then it will be the next therapist, who is also an OT, and that's it: then she will be the only OT left."

This information, along with the swiveling, confused and upset me. I could not imagine anyone would be so underhanded, especially my supervisor. I thought we had a good relationship. I wanted to believe that she would try to find me a position elsewhere. Didn't she have my best interests at heart?

I heeded his advice, however. The next morning, after a sleepless night, I called the union, to no avail. Apparently my representative was in meetings, so I left a number of messages. The social worker, his comforting presence steady as a rock, urged me to keep calling. "Bug him, he has to return your call. That is his job." While he stacked his papers together preparing for a visit, he added that I should document everything my supervisor said to me about leaving, and also record the dates and times I called the union. His solid and comforting presence in our cubicle, something I had always enjoyed, had now become invaluable. Heeding his advice, I kept notes on every conversation and phone call. Besides those notes, I still had my evaluations and follow-up forms to write, but I was no longer as diligent as I had been, because it didn't seem to matter. Why should I push myself when no one cared?

After about four weeks, someone called, identifying himself as my union representative. I was stunned when I heard this, and so scared that the voice would evaporate that I quickly told him what had transpired over these past weeks. I presumed he was listening, because he was quiet for the length of my outburst. When I finished he replied that neither the union nor the county's personnel department had been informed of these impending changes. Reiterating what the social worker had said, he assured me I could not be terminated unless the union had been informed, and no other position had been found. He promised to find out what was happening and call me back.

In the meantime, my supervisor had returned from her vacation, looking rested and tanned. A day later she called me to her desk, clicked her pen, jiggled her foot, and said she had made inquiries in all the county departments, and there were definitely no openings for a therapist.

"You must look outside the county," she said, and the fog that had swirled around me when she first spoke to me returned. Click, jiggle. "I have no idea when these changes will happen, but it is probably quite soon, the next month or so." For clarity's sake she added, "In other words, you will be laid off. As I told you: last hired, first fired. Of course, for the time being just keep on working."

I had neither the energy nor desire to look for another position anywhere, either in or out of the county, so I continued to work in limbo, pretending everything was just fine. I also didn't hear anything from the union. The stripper was fast becoming a confidante, but I was only allowed two visits after my initial evaluation. How could I really be of service, to her or to anyone? This was not what I had imagined when I began working in home health. I thought we cared about the sick and needy—after all, my supervisor constantly reminded me that the head of Public Health was absolutely dedicated to serving all the residents of the county. He placed a tremendous importance on our services, she said, and emphasized this at administration meetings.

Now, because of the cuts, all the people who had been so dedicated were worried about losing their jobs, and no one voiced any concern about the consumers/patients. Who would see them if we could not? Would they be deserted? Left to fend for themselves?

Even after my visits to the stripper ended, we spoke to each other over the phone, and I popped by if I was in the vicinity of her home. Something about this fascinating woman's sense of humor, her acceptance of the ways of the world, and her indomitable spirit buoyed my flagging spirits. Our roles had reversed; wasn't I supposed to be helping her? When I told her about the new rules and regulations, she tut-tutted, saying that is how systems are. "They make no sense, no sense at all." Over a salad I brought for us to share, she wanted to speak of other matters. Was I married? She hoped not, because she adored her doctor, who she thought was divorced, and she wanted us to meet. How could she be thinking of such mundane matters, I wondered, when she was obviously becoming increasingly ill? Her flesh sagged alarmingly under her high cheekbones, and she became an even more ashy gray. Her collarbones stood out sharply. Although she never used the word cancer, we both knew she had lung cancer in an advanced stage.

Desks have ears, and walls have eyes. Everyone, it seemed, from home health aides to clerks, knew that my position was on the line. Everyone had well-meaning advice. I was bombarded by every single person I had ever crossed paths with, either as they walked by my desk or when I saw them in the bathroom, hallways, or around the coffee stand. Each and every one said that my supervisor belonged to administration and therefore badmouthed the union. Administration cannot just get rid of us. The reality was that administration was hell-bent on getting rid of me. All this well-intended advice only caused the fog around me to thicken. I promised to read the Memorandum of Understanding between the union and its members. Halfheartedly, I began looking in occupational therapy journals and newspapers to see what was available outside the county. I went about my days in a state of confusion. My enthusiasm for work waned. I was hurt and angry. Why should I put all my time and energy into an organization that cared about the health and well-being of neither their own employees nor the population they served?

Up went my stress level. I had a hard time sleeping and felt so exhausted I had no idea how I drove home every day without nodding off at the wheel. I was endangering everyone on the streets and the freeways. Between the fog, the stress, and my hormones, which had begun playing havoc, I was either in a state of homicidal anger, primed to cause grave bodily harm to anyone who offended me, or ready to burst into uncontrollable sobbing at any given moment. I knew I was seriously losing it, whatever it was, when one morning I was reduced to a puddle at the sight of an elderly patient carrying his garbage to the recycling bin outside his home.

Our collective productivity was down because we hardly received referrals. Every morning, yet another nurse stopped by my desk to say she'd found a new placement within the county. They were lucky; there seemed to be tons of work for nurses, both within and outside county employment. Until about a year ago it had been like that for therapists. Now, thanks to new rules, placements were drying up. Occupational therapy was no longer one of the most in-demand jobs of the 1990s. Then the unthinkable happened. Big Bill told me he would be leaving soon for another position in the county health system. Oh, how I would miss him, his boots, his earring, his food, and his stories. The patients would also miss him. Everything seemed to come tumbling down in our house of cards. Two home health aides took early retirement while a third began work elsewhere. We could no longer refer aides to assist patients with their exercises and bathing. Furthermore, my supervisor informed us that Medicare had denied payment for many of our visits. Rumors flew that the agency would close down, or that all offices would be moved to one centralized hub in Martinez, to save still more rent on office space. No longer would I enjoy the sanctuary of our cubicle, and anyway, there was hardly anyone left for me to talk to.

By now patients were well aware of the changes and they were upset, angry, and scared. Rightfully, they felt they had no voice in their care. It was as if the planets had lost their orbits, and we, with them, were whirling helplessly in space.

Early one morning I happened to see the stripper in the county health clinic. She had come in to see her doctor. Although we had spoken over the phone, I hadn't seen her for quite a few weeks, and I was shocked by her appearance. She looked so thin and frail I was afraid to hug her, but immediately she put her arms around me. I sat with her while she waited for her doctor.

"I have cancer, honey," she said in her increasingly raspy voice. "I don't have much longer. What are you doing right now? Do you have time to stay with me and meet the doctor?" She winked conspiratorially. Unfortunately, I didn't have time. That was the last time I saw her. A month or two later I had occasion to call her doctor about another patient. I asked him how she was and he informed me that she had "expired."

In February, before I heard from the union representative, the supervisor of the early intervention program for infants with

special needs based in another area of Richmond called to say
he had heard what was happening. Of course he had, he was
part of administration. He told me he knew the county had no
open positions for occupational therapists, but he could offer me
a temporary position working in the Early Intervention Program in Concord. A departmental aide was needed, not a therapist, but I could "fill in" as a consultant while I "helped" in the
program. After some deliberation, I accepted his offer—reluctantly, because I did not feel competent working with infants,
having worked with adults for so long. Another reason was that
a pediatric home-based therapist who worked in Richmond in
early intervention with children from zero to three years old had
confided to me that she planned to leave soon and encouraged
me to take her place. She had not yet informed her supervisor
of her plans but would do so shortly. Her suggestion contained
a ray of hope. It was something I thought I might enjoy, especially as she worked in the children's homes, which I knew I
would like. Of course this too would be a challenge, requiring
me to learn a new field, but that could be exciting. It was with
her position in mind that I agreed to work in Concord; I thought
I could bear anything in the meantime.

My last day in home health was a Friday. My supervisor, who
had been informed of my move and knew this was my last day,
was nowhere to be seen, nor did she phone to check in, as she
always did. Instead, she left me notes about whom to see that
day. She included a new evaluation, which I knew, and she knew,
would take a couple of hours, and afterward even more time to
complete the paperwork. I could not complete that in a day. I was
furious, because this was patently unfair. Fortunately, the patient
was not at home when I called, and they did not have an answer-
ing machine. This fortuitous event lifted my spirits somewhat.

The per diem physical therapist was not at work. I was unable
to contact the two therapists who worked in East County, both
next in line to be laid off. I had wanted to say good-bye to them.
I'd heard reports over the office gossip mill that the therapist
above me on the seniority list was extremely stressed and fearful

about losing her position. Rumors about workers hiring lawyers were prevalent, and the word "sue" was frequently used, but I really dislike that word and all it implies, and I had not asked more about it. Not even the social worker was there on my last day, but we had said our farewells previously. He too was taking another position.

I saw the required 4.5 patients and completed my paperwork. At the end of the day I placed my paperwork in the inbox on the clerks' desk, along with my beeper. Everyone had left for the day. I looked around the office. It was full of ghosts. I turned around, removed my car keys from my handbag, and walked out. Eight years were over. On Monday I would begin the temporary position in Concord.

CHAPTER 43

During the few months I worked in Concord, I felt as if I had been punched in my diaphragm, and my life force and enthusiasm dissipated. I did not enjoy spending my days diapering tiny children, washing faces and hands, and brushing teeth. I, who had been tired of the relentless pace of change, now felt that time was stagnant; nothing changed between waking, working, and returning home. Every day was consumed by the same unfulfilling motions. It was like moving between a few enormous stone edifices, in, out, around, repeating the same tasks. My mind remained in the dense, drizzly fog that constantly accompanied me. I felt like a cartoon character, slumped over, head bent down, dark cloud overhead. Occasionally, especially on the drive to and from Concord, I thought of all those years I studied in Jerusalem. I remembered taking my licensing exams to work in America. The eight years I had worked in home health evaporated. The fog obliterated any feelings of accomplishment and extinguished any vestige of hope. I was scared, and I felt that I had not accomplished anything. I was worthless, unsuited for anything other than diapering infants, and apparently I was not quick enough at that, either. I started out thinking I worked in a caring environment, but I learned that everything revolves around money. Since when had my self-worth become so entangled with my work? How had I allowed this to happen to me, the hardy survivor? Had life turned me into a wimp?

After a couple of months of changing diapers and fruitlessly calling the union, I was surprised one day, while wrestling a coat onto a little boy, to receive a phone call. Someone who identified himself as being from the union informed me that "We are behind you all the way." My mouth hung open in shocked silence as he continued, "Not one of you therapists will lose your place in the county."

I zipped up the boy's coat and sat down, holding the phone in my hand and gaping at the receiver. I was unable to say anything sensible at all, like "Where have you been for the last four months?"

The voice continued. "There will be a meeting with you and the other occupational therapist who is slated to be 'terminated,' the administration, Human Resources (whoever they were), and the union."

I felt my heart thudding as the voice went on. "We will meet at the County Building next Tuesday at 4.30 p.m. I will be in the lobby before the meeting. Come and speak to me then."

I remained sitting, forgetting that there were three other children to be diapered. What is more, I didn't give a damn. Not once had I worked as a therapist in this setting. A well-trained monkey could probably diaper a child more efficiently and quickly than I could. What had caused this sudden attention? Had someone said the word "sue" one too many times? Oh well, I would go to the meeting and hear what was said.

The following Tuesday, we met in the lobby at the appointed time. The gray-haired, overweight, short-of-breath representative explained to me that in the upcoming meeting he would lay out union rules, and inform administration of how these had been transgressed. While he spoke, the next therapist on the firing line rushed in, looking as drawn and haggard as I surely did. Until she had learned that she would be the next to leave, she had barely acknowledged my anguish, probably because she felt ashamed that I had to go. Now she stood next to me and tearfully whispered that she understood how I must feel.

After the meeting began, the representative spoke in union legalese, explaining that the county should have informed them of upcoming changes before putting them into place. According to union rules, we were supposed to be transferred to new placements, retaining our seniority and, of course, our positions as therapists. Nobody could make us transfer without informing the union. After a lengthy discourse in which all sides laid out their positions, we, the therapists, were asked to relate what had transpired. I told them in no uncertain terms that my position in home health had been terminated, and I was now working as an aide in Concord. The other therapist tearfully insisted that she would only work in home health, because that was her area of expertise, she had put years of work into the field, and she could not just go and work elsewhere.

Administration took time out for a caucus. With grave faces they returned to say that there were no longer any positions open in home health. They asked to meet again in two weeks' time, during which they would confer with department heads as to other available positions. Because the other therapist had seniority over me, she could choose any placement that was offered before I could. Two more weeks of bending over to pick little ones up. Two more weeks of wiping noses and bottoms and putting on diapers. Two more weeks of a zombie-like, fog-enshrouded existence.

After the fortnight was over, we returned to the County Building for our next meeting. By now I was feeling nothing but a white-hot anger steaming up inside of me, threatening to boil over at any time, and I was scared of what I might say or do. I sat around the conference table glaring at everyone present. The other therapist sat next to me, silently crying, dabbing at her eyes and cheeks.

A department head cleared his throat, sipped from a bottle of water, then said they had looked around the county government and had spoken with all the other department heads and supervisors. They were pleased to inform us that there were three positions that they could offer us. One was my present position in Concord. Between clenched teeth I informed them that this is not a placement for an occupational therapist. The man from the union agreed with me, reaffirming that it was for an aide, not a therapist, unless the duties are reassigned. Undeterred, and without responding to me, the head again cleared his throat, then said the second position was in the geriatric psychiatric ward in the county hospital. The other therapist and I sat there looking at each other in shock, then turned our faces away, each trying to digest this information while we waited to hear about the third position. This was the one I hoped for, the pediatric home-based therapist position in Richmond. While I glared and the other woman sniffled, and the union representative beamed because he had fulfilled the union's promises to its members, the department head stated we had yet another two weeks' time in which to consider these life-changing positions. We would reconvene on the specified date to inform them of our decisions.

Exhausted, with the fog again descending heavily over me, seeping into every cell of my brain and my being, clashing with the anger, I hauled myself into my car to drive the now extremely familiar route from Martinez to Albany. As I shifted into fourth gear, my mind wandered back over the last eight years of work. Then it drifted further back, to Israel. I remembered the reason I had decided to study OT in the first place: the pregnancies that had made me depend on the help of others, and the terrible war that had shattered my life; the desire to make this world a little less of a burden. Despite all I have seen, and the manner in which I have been treated, it still seems to me that anything I can do to alleviate suffering, either my own or that of others, is the only thing worth living for.

Driving through the rolling hills, I remembered the interesting, desperate, brave, crazy people I had met over the last eight years. I realized how much I had learned about America, and certainly Contra Costa County, and the varied peoples who make up its population. I remembered sad, intense, touching, funny times, and those moments when I really connected with patients. I remembered their radiant smiles, the warm feeling that fills my being when I see changes, the simple touch that conveys far more than words. I remembered seeing Sally Ann when she was at the clinic for a doctor's visit. She was being helped out of a taxi just as I walked out to the parking lot. She saw me, and her pallid face lit up briefly with a rare smile as she beckoned me to come and hug her. A week before Christmas one year, I had driven past the home of the man whose neighbor, the retired football player, had helped him in and out of his tub. He was strolling down the street, using his quad cane. I stopped to say hi, even though it had been a few years since I had seen him. "Hey," he said, smiling. "So good to see you, come here for a hug. Come see my wife, she'll be glad to see you." I thought of the addicts I had met who did change their lives and were now helping others, as counselors and sponsors. They rebuilt the ties that had been shattered by their addictions and returned from the abyss to reclaim their children, their families, their friends, their health. I remembered the victims of violence who overcame their loss and horror to assist others. I am filled with awe at the bravery of women who, without education or money, put their faith in God, left abusive husbands, and rebuilt their lives. It was then, on that familiar twenty-minute drive from Martinez, that I remembered I had touched people's lives, and they mine. Those eight years did mean something to me, as well as to those with whom I had worked—human beings, not consumers.

I thought of the nurses, the aides, the clerks, and all we had shared; marriages, illnesses, deaths, divorce. My mouth watered as I remembered the potlucks, the scrumptious homemade ice cream—coffee, mango, ginger, and vanilla from Madagascar. Succulent slices of roast turkey, salads of wild rice and pine nuts, melt-in-your-mouth buttery cookies, layered cheesecakes. All of us had lost, we had all been hurt, but instead of comforting each other we had shut down our hearts and walked away, concerned about our immediate present and the frightening picture of a future without benefits.

I drove into the bank of fog engulfing the East Bay. Suddenly, after months of living in my own dense fog, the sun's rays emerged through my personal overhanging cloud, touching me, and my heart, and filling my car with a blazing warmth that penetrated the surrounding gloom. At the very instant that the warmth extinguished the anger, I knew exactly what I wanted. I would ask for the position working in early intervention in Richmond. If the other therapist decides to choose that placement, I thought, knowing full well she could do that, I will leave the county, I will find something else, and I know I will be fine. To contribute to others is my reason for being here. Because of this work, I no longer feel like a stranger in a strange land, separate from all that surrounds me. Although I will always remember and dream about South Africa and Israel, I feel that, like Mae's, my roots have taken hold, and they are growing strong in this new and different land.

EPILOGUE

As the French say, "The more things change, the more they stay the same."

The home health agency is no more. The other occupational therapist decided against working in Richmond. She no longer works in home health, but compromised on a suitable part-time position in the county, closer to her home. I accepted the position in Richmond, and the occupational therapist who worked there did leave. For a couple of years everything seemed fine, and then once more the process of budget cuts and eliminating positions began. Once again I and others who worked in West County found ourselves sitting at meetings with the union and administration. Most people, for very sound reasons, wanted to continue as county employees and took other placements. I was not one of them. I did not have the heart to continue under changing conditions that, in the end, would remain the same: i.e., our program would close.

I now do the same work, with infants, for a nonprofit organization that took over for the flailing, flailing, flailed county, which is "no longer in the business of taking care of the needy."

Over the years I have bumped into many of my former patients, and it has always been a pleasant reunion, especially when they are doing well. I am constantly amazed that they remember me. Many times I run across family members of deceased patients, and we always find time for a chat. Unfortunately, I still find names of people I know in the newspapers, and I still attend untimely funerals. I have kept in touch with some of the nurses and home health aides. We still meet and gossip over margaritas.

I go to Israel yearly, and I recently went back to South Africa, where I reconnected with family and friends. It is indeed the new South Africa, no longer a source of shame and disgrace but one of vital change, hope, and pride. The moment the plane I am in touches down in these two homes, my American side seems to diminish. It is as if the years or months since I was back in these countries collapse like a concertina. In South Africa I was stunned to find that the home in which I grew up, with its wonderful garden and trees, has been razed to the ground. Condos will go up in its place. The mulberry tree is no more.

Although my roots still miss the red South African soil, I no longer feel uprooted. The roots I grew there are a deep source of comfort and nourishment for me, wherever I am.

About the Author

Lawrence Migdale/Pix

Born and raised in Johannesburg, South Africa, Nesta Rovina received a degree from Rhodes University in Grahamstown. She lived in Israel for eleven years, eight of them on Kibbutz Ein Dor. She received her degree in occupational therapy in Jerusalem and has lived and worked in the Bay Area since 1980. She has an MA from John F. Kennedy University in Orinda and has had essays published locally and in England.

Other BayTree Books

BayTree Books, a project of Heyday Institute, gives voice to a full range of California experience and personal stories.

The Oracles: My Filipino Grandparents in America (2006)
Pati Navalta Poblete

Fast Cars and Frybread: Reports from the Rez (2007)
Gordon Johnson

Ticket to Exile (2007)
Adam David Miller

Archy Lee: A California Fugitive Slave Case (2008)
Rudolph M. Lapp

Walking Tractor: And Other Country Tales (2008)
Bruce Patterson

Where Light Takes Its Color from the Sea:
A California Notebook (2008)
James D. Houston

BAYTREE

HEYDAY INSTITUTE

Since its founding in 1974, Heyday Books has occupied a unique niche in the publishing world, specializing in books that foster an understanding of the history, literature, art, environment, social issues, and culture of California and the West. We are a 501(c)(3) nonprofit organization based in Berkeley, California, serving a wide range of people and audiences.

We are grateful for the generous funding we've received for our publications and programs during the past year from foundations and more than three hundred individual donors. Major supporters include:

Anonymous; Anthony Andreas, Jr.; Barnes & Noble bookstores; BayTree Fund; B.C.W. Trust III; S. D. Bechtel, Jr. Foundation; Fred & Jean Berensmeier; Book Club of California; Butler Koshland Fund; California Council for the Humanities; California State Coastal Conservancy; California State Library; Candelaria Fund; Columbia Foundation; Compton Foundation, Inc.; Malcolm Cravens Foundation; Federated Indians of Graton Rancheria; Fleishhacker Foundation; Wallace Alexander Gerbode Foundation; Marion E. Greene; Walter & Elise Haas Fund; Leanne Hinton; Hopland Band of Pomo Indians; James Irvine Foundation; George Frederick Jewett Foundation; Marty Krasney; Guy Lampard & Suzanne Badenhoop; LEF Foundation; Robert Levitt; Michael McCone; Middletown Rancheria Tribal Council; National Audubon Society; National Endowment for the Arts; National Park Service; Philanthropic Ventures Foundation; Poets & Writers; Rim of the World Interpretive Association; River Rock Casino; Riverside-Corona Resource Conservation; Alan Rosenus; San Francisco Foundation; Santa Ana Watershed Association; William Saroyan Foundation; Seaver Institute; Sandy Cold Shapero; Service Plus Credit Union; L. J. Skaggs & Mary C. Skaggs Foundation; Skirball Foundation; Orin Starn; Swinerton Family Fund; Thendara Foundation; Victorian Alliance; Tom White; Harold & Alma White Memorial Fund; and Stan Yogi.

For more information about Heyday Institute, our publications and programs, please visit our website at www.heydaybooks.com.